STUDY GUIDE

LEVERAGE
YOUR LEGACY

**USING TEMPORAL WEALTH
FOR ETERNAL GAIN**

KENNETH BOA & RUSS CROSSON
with **BRETT EASTMAN**

Copyright © 2024 by Kenneth Boa and Russ Crosson with Brett Eastman

ALL RIGHTS RESERVED

Copyright and use of the curriculum template is retained by Brett Eastman.

Unless otherwise noted, all Scripture quotes are taken from The Holy Bible, English Standard Version. ESV® Text Edition: 2016. Copyright ©2001 by Crossway Bibles, a publishing ministry of Good News Publishers.

ISBN: 978-1-950007-99-8

Printed in the United States of America

Contents

i.	Foreword
ii.	Welcome
iii.	Endorsements
13	Special Acknowledgment
14	Introduction
16	Using this Workbook
17	Outline for Each Session

GROUP SESSIONS

20	1: Introduction | Exploring the Principles & Practices of Leverage
34	2: Why Are We to Give? | Importance of Accountability
48	3: When Are We to Give? | Current vs. Deferred Giving
62	4: How Are We to Give? | Cash Flow vs. Net Worth Giving
76	5: How Much Are We to Give? | Finding the Finish Line
90	6: Where Are We to Give? | Estate Planning & Foundations

APPENDICES

106	Frequently Asked Questions
110	Small Group Agreement
112	Small Group Calendar
113	Small Group Roster
114	Weekly Check In
115	Memory Verse Cards
117	Prayer & Praise Report

SMALL GROUP LEADERS

118	Hosting an Open House
120	Leading for the First Time
121	Leadership Training
125	Acknowledgements
126	Next Steps

Foreword

For over 40 years as pastor of Saddleback Church, I've seen firsthand how lives are transformed when people embrace a purpose-driven life—one that is focused on contributing to God's Kingdom rather than just accumulating wealth. One of the greatest callings we have as believers is to be faithful stewards of the resources God entrusts to us. But stewardship isn't just about managing wealth—it's about using it to make an eternal impact and fulfilling the Great Commission.

That's why I'm excited about this new Leverage curriculum and study guide, which follows the powerful principles laid out in the Leverage book by Ken Boa and Russ Crosson. This guide is not just a companion—it's a practical tool designed to help you apply the concepts of biblical stewardship, generosity, and legacy-building in a personal and profound way. Whether you are leading a small group, facilitating discussions in your church, or working with families of wealth, this study guide will bring the truths of Leverage to life.

Through beautifully produced and creatively crafted media, the teachings, training, and testimonies come to life in ways you've never seen before. The experiential study guide will lead you to take what you've learned and apply it not only in your life but also in your family, ministry, business, and hopefully, your church. Our vision is to see small groups launched in every church across the country, creating a ripple effect of generosity and family legacy, especially among families of wealth. Will you join us in this journey?

This curriculum provides access to the most comprehensive digital library designed to support you every step of the way. Whether you're a family member, church leader, small group host, senior pastor, financial advisor, or nonprofit leader, we have a playbook and pathway to guide you on this transformative journey.

With the help of videos, testimonies, and group discussions, this guide will equip you to take what you've learned and apply it in your own life, your family, and your church. Jesus called us to store up treasures in Heaven, and this curriculum will help you take that call seriously. It's more than a study—it's an invitation to live a purpose-driven life that maximizes the impact of what God has entrusted to you.

I encourage you to go through this guide with an open heart, ready to see how God can use your time, talents, and treasures for His Kingdom. Russ and Ken, along with Brett, have given us a remarkable resource, and I believe it will lead to transformation not only in your life but in the lives of everyone you touch.

RICK WARREN

Author of *The Purpose Driven Life*,
Founding Pastor of Saddleback Church
& *Finishing the Task* Coalition

Welcome

Dear Friends,

Welcome to the Leverage journey! We are thrilled that you've chosen to explore this curriculum, a companion to the book ***Leverage: Using Temporal Wealth for Eternal Gain***. Whether you're a pastor, financial advisor, or part of a ministry, this study is designed to be a transformative tool for you, your church and the families you serve.

This curriculum will guide you through six focused sessions on biblical principles of stewardship, generosity and legacy-building. We encourage you to dive into the robust video content—including session videos, tips, and inspiring testimonies—accessible through the QR codes in this study guide. These resources will further enrich your discussions and deepen your understanding of how to use temporal wealth for eternal purposes.

As you engage with the study, use the guide as both a resource and a conversation starter for your group. The daily devotions and reading plan are designed to help you reflect on and apply these principles in your life. Together, we hope this journey will help you leverage the gifts God has given for His greater glory.

We look forward to walking alongside you in this exciting journey of stewardship and eternal impact.

In Christ,

KENNETH BOA, RUSS CROSSON & BRETT EASTMAN

Endorsements

"It gives me great pleasure to endorse this curriculum, and I endorse it because of the two men who conceived and constructed it. I know few people who are so committed to truth and believe that God provides wisdom for every financial decision and every decision in life. Russ and Ken are two Giants of Faith and I endorse them in this curriculum with total confidence of its powerful message that will transform lives."

RON BLUE, Personal Finance Author and Founder of Blue Trust, Kingdom Advisors, and the Ron Blue Institute

"I'm grateful for Ken Boa and Russ Crosson writing their book, *Leverage*, which provides very practical ways of living and giving generously. What a blessing to also have this interactive study guide and video-based curriculum to encourage each of us in our own financial stewardship & generosity journey as we hear inspiring stories from people who are leveraging their time, talents, treasure, and influence to bring more of God's Kingdom here on Earth as it is in Heaven."

MARK BATTERSON, New York Times Bestselling Author of *The Circle Maker*; Lead Pastor of National Community Church

"Many aspire to be generous—when they're older, wealthier, or more established—but whatever our phase of life, generosity begins now in the way we steward our time, talent, and treasure. As we grow in generosity, we will undoubtedly find that what is good for the world around us is also good for our soul. I'm grateful for the dynamic partnership between theologian Ken Boa and practitioner Russ Crosson and their impactful new book, Leverage, that will undoubtedly help us grow into greater generosity."

PETER GREER, President and CEO of Hope International; Co-Author of *Mission Drift*

"This incredible curriculum called Leverage is helping men, women and families of wealth make the very most of their possessions for eternal purposes."

John Maxwell, No. 1 New York Times bestselling author, coach, speaker and leadership authority

"What a wonderful joy and privilege to be a part of the *Leverage* series. The focus of this important resource is on the faithful stewardship of the resources God places in our hands in such a way that leaves a legacy of generosity while placing the spotlight on lasting, eternal values. This is such an important, timely, and helpful gift. So grateful for the emphasis and message of the Leverage series!"

DR. CRAWFORD W. LORITTS, JR., Author, Speaker, Radio Host; President, Beyond our Generation

"Russ Crosson and Blue Trust have managed my assets for over 25 years, and Ken Boa has discipled my mind & my heart for decades. I can't think of a better team to help us grasp the sheer genius of generosity for all of life and every relationship. I highly recommend the proven teaching and truth found in their breakthrough book and curriculum, Leverage."

CHIP INGRAM, CEO and Teaching Pastor, Living on the Edge

"As a philanthropy lawyer, I regularly encounter clients that have committed to their legacy gifts at the end of their lives, but they are unfulfilled in terms of the impact of their giving during their lives. I appreciate the tools that Russ Crosson and Ken Boa have created with Leverage and this study guide to help families create a giving plan, specific priorities, and a shared commitment for family generosity. The *Leverage Study Guide* will put practical tools in the hands of families to live a generous life today, with an eternal mindset."

MARILEE J. SPRINGER, Attorney, Blue Trust Board Member

"I believe that anyone investing their time in this curriculum will be greatly rewarded. Russ and Ken lead the seeker to a greater understanding of how they can live generously and in so doing can enrich their life and the lives of others."

JANET VAUGHAN, a 40+ year Blue Trust client

"I think the biggest takeaway from *Leverage* is the impact that it can have for different generations of the family. It could be used as a system to have that conversation with families and get them on a pathway to success. As they said, if that conversation doesn't take place while they're alive, it's going to take place in a lawyer's office."

EDDIE BEAL, Compliance Manager at Blue Trust

"I have been friends with Russ Crosson for many years and have witnessed personally his heart and ability to communicate the need and reality of what Generosity in people's lives could look like! The work that he and Ken have done is exceptional, and I have given many books to many people that need to consider how to leverage their generosity to impact this world. Our generation is coming into tremendous wealth that many definitely will not need. This book helps move hearts towards considering how to best leverage what God has given them and invest their life and resources in what is eternal, the kingdom of God."

DON ANKENBRANDT, Director of Generous Life Alabama, Founder of Alliance Ministries (a Halftime coaching organization)

"Typically, pastors have a heart to help but they are just not so sure how to approach it because they don't really teach this money stuff in seminary. We now have a resource in Leverage that can help any pastor or congregation. This series has a not only sound theological foundation, but also some very helpful and practical applications to encourage those with a little or a lot in your congregations."

BRIAN SHEPLER, President/CEO of Blue Trust

I have known Ken and Russ for many years and I highly recommend you read *Leverage* and participate in their study. They do a masterful job of handling both the WHY and the HOW of giving. Ken brings the Biblical truths about giving and Russ brings the practical and tax efficient ways to help you steward what God has entrusted to you. If you want to build a legacy of generosity in your family, you will learn much from their book and study.

TOM CONWAY, Founder & CEO of Family Legacy By Design

Special Acknowledgment

We would like to make a special acknowledgment to Brett Eastman, the Founder and President of *LifeTogether*. He approached us with immense encouragement and foresight, consistently reminding us that "this content is gold and needs to be in the churches." Brett and his team did an outstanding job not only filming the town hall content but also synthesizing various inputs to create a curriculum that is both engaging and informative for all readers.

Brett Eastman founded LifeTogether Ministries over 25 years ago and served as the Small Group Champion at Willow Creek Community Church and at Saddleback Church with Rick Warren, where he helped to develop the 40 Days of Purpose Campaign and wrote the Purpose Driven Small Group series with Zondervan, which sold over 5 million copies.

At *LifeTogether*, Brett consulted and produced resources with over 5,000 churches and published and produced over 500 video curriculum and church campaigns. Brett is co-founder of *Legacy By Design*, helping to coach families of wealth navigate the challenges of family life and legacy. In addition, Brett has started a new venture, *Family Legacy Productions*, helping to bring your family story, values, and legacy to life.

Introduction

In the 3rd century BC, Archimedes, a renowned Greek scholar, articulated a powerful principle: "Effort times effort arm equals load times load arm." This concept, originally applied to physical mechanics, introduces us to the notion of leverage. What exactly is an "effort arm"? Simply put, it's a lever—a tool that amplifies our effort to move a load.

Archimedes famously declared, "Give me a lever long enough and a fulcrum on which to place it, and I will move the world." Could this profound principle extend beyond physical applications into the realm of spiritual truths?

Indeed, the principle has been applied many times to non-physical ideas. A lever could be a new skill, an interest rate, a piece of intellectual property, or someone's leadership ability. But in this series, esteemed theologian Ken Boa and financial expert Russ Crosson will unpack an idea that Jesus introduced in His enigmatic parable of the servant who used his master's money to gain for himself friends in the afterlife. Luke 16:9 says, "And I tell you, make friends for yourselves by means of unrighteous wealth, so that when it fails they may receive you into the eternal dwellings." Jesus saw using one's money as a lever for spiritual growth and reward.

The *Leverage Study Guide* distills decades of theological insight and financial wisdom into a transformative curriculum. This course illuminates God's perspective on generosity and its profound role within His Kingdom, and specifically how both we and God use our wealth as a lever in this process.

Across six comprehensive sessions, you will embark on a journey of discovery.

1. Introduction: Exploring the Principles & Practices of Leverage

2. Why Are We to Give?: Importance of Accountability

3. When Are We to Give?: Current vs. Deferred Giving

4. How Are We to Give?: Cash Flow vs. Net Worth Giving

5. How Much Are We to Give?: Finding the Finish Line

6. Where Are We to Give?: Estate Planning & Foundations

By the conclusion of this empowering series, you will not only gain a profound understanding of biblical teachings on generosity but also practical strategies to leverage your resources for eternal impact in God's Kingdom.

Using this Workbook

TOOLS TO HELP YOU HAVE A GREAT SMALL GROUP EXPERIENCE:

1. Notice in the Table of Contents there are three sections: 1) Sessions; 2) Appendices; and 3) Small Group Leaders. Familiarize yourself with the Appendices. Some of them will be used in the sessions themselves.

2. If you are facilitating/leading or co-leading a small group, the section titled Small Group Leaders will give you some insights of others that will encourage you and help you avoid many common obstacles to effective small group leadership.

3. Use this workbook as a guide, not a straitjacket. If the group responds to the lesson in an unexpected but honest way, go with that. If you think of a better question than the next one in the lesson, ask it. Take to heart the insights included in the Frequently Asked Questions and the Small Group Leaders sections.

4. Enjoy your small group experience.

5. Pray before each session—for your group members, for your time together, and for wisdom and insights.

6. Read the outline for each session on the next pages so that you understand how the sessions will flow.

Outline of Each Session

A typical group session for the *Leverage Study Guide* will include the following sections. Read through this to get a clear idea of how each group meeting will be structured:

WEEKLY MEMORY VERSES. Each session opens with a Memory Verse that emphasizes an important truth from the session. This exercise is optional, but we believe that memorizing Scripture can be a vital part of filling our minds with God's Word for our lives. We encourage you to give this important habit a try. The verses for our six sessions are also listed in the Appendices.

PRAYER. Remember that the group should first open in prayer. This prayer should be brief, simple, and invite God to provide insight as you work through the study.

ICEBREAKER. The foundation for spiritual growth is an intimate connection with God and His family. You build that connection by sharing your story with a few people who really know you and who have earned your trust. This section includes some simple questions to get the group members talking—letting individuals share as much or as little of their story as they feel comfortable doing. Each session typically offers two options: 1) you can get to know the whole group by using the icebreaker question(s), or 2) you can check in with one or two group members for a deeper connection and encouragement in their spiritual journey.

WATCH. Weekly you'll have the opportunity to join esteemed theologian Kenneth Boa, financial expert Russ Crosson and dynamic host, Brett Eastman, as they walk you through key principles and practices to distill decades of theological insight and financial wisdom into a transformative curriculum. All you'll need to do is scan the QR Code or select the link to watch the video session.

SCAN or go to
leverageyourlegacy.org

DISCUSSION. In this section, you'll have the opportunity to read passages of Scripture and discuss both the video teaching and text. You won't focus on accumulating information but rather on how you should live in light of the Word of God. We want to help you apply the insights from Scripture practically and creatively, from your heart as well as your head. At the end of the day, our greatest aim should be to allow the timeless truths from God's Word to transform our lives in Christ.

APPLICATION. God wants you to be a part of His Kingdom—to weave your story into His. That will mean change. It will require you to go His way rather than your own. This won't happen overnight, but it should happen steadily. By making small, simple choices, we can begin to change our direction. This is where the Bible's instructions to be doers of the Word, not just hearers (James 1:22) comes into play. Many people skip over this aspect of the Christian life because it's scary, relationally awkward, or simply too much work for their busy schedules. But Jesus wanted all of His disciples to know Him personally, carry out His commands, and help outsiders connect with Him. This doesn't necessarily mean preaching on street corners. It could mean going deeper into this topic of generosity. Each week, you can do so by meditating on the application questions, reading the daily devotions, praying, journaling, following the reading plan, or exploring what others have done in this area. In this study, you'll have an opportunity to go beyond Bible study to biblical living.

OUTLINE OF EACH SESSION

DAILY DEVOTIONS. Each week on the Daily Devotions pages, we provide Scriptures to read and reflect on between sessions. This provides you with a chance to slow down, read just a small portion of Scripture each day, and reflect and pray through it. You'll then have a chance to journal your response to what you've read. Use this section to seek God on your own throughout the week. This time at home should begin and end with prayer. Don't get in a hurry; take enough time to hear God's direction.

READING PLAN. To reinforce the principles in the video teaching, you are encouraged to read through the *Leverage: Using Temporal Wealth for Eternal Gain* book. A weekly reading plan is offered for Sessions 2-6 that correspond to that session's teaching.

EXPLORE. You'll also have the opportunity to read, view, and listen to inspiring *Faces of Generosity* and/or *Leverage* stories, proven tips and best practices to help you apply the timeless principles and practices of leverage. You'll simply select a QR code or link to experience these dynamic elements of this curriculum.

SCAN or go to
leverageyourlegacy.org

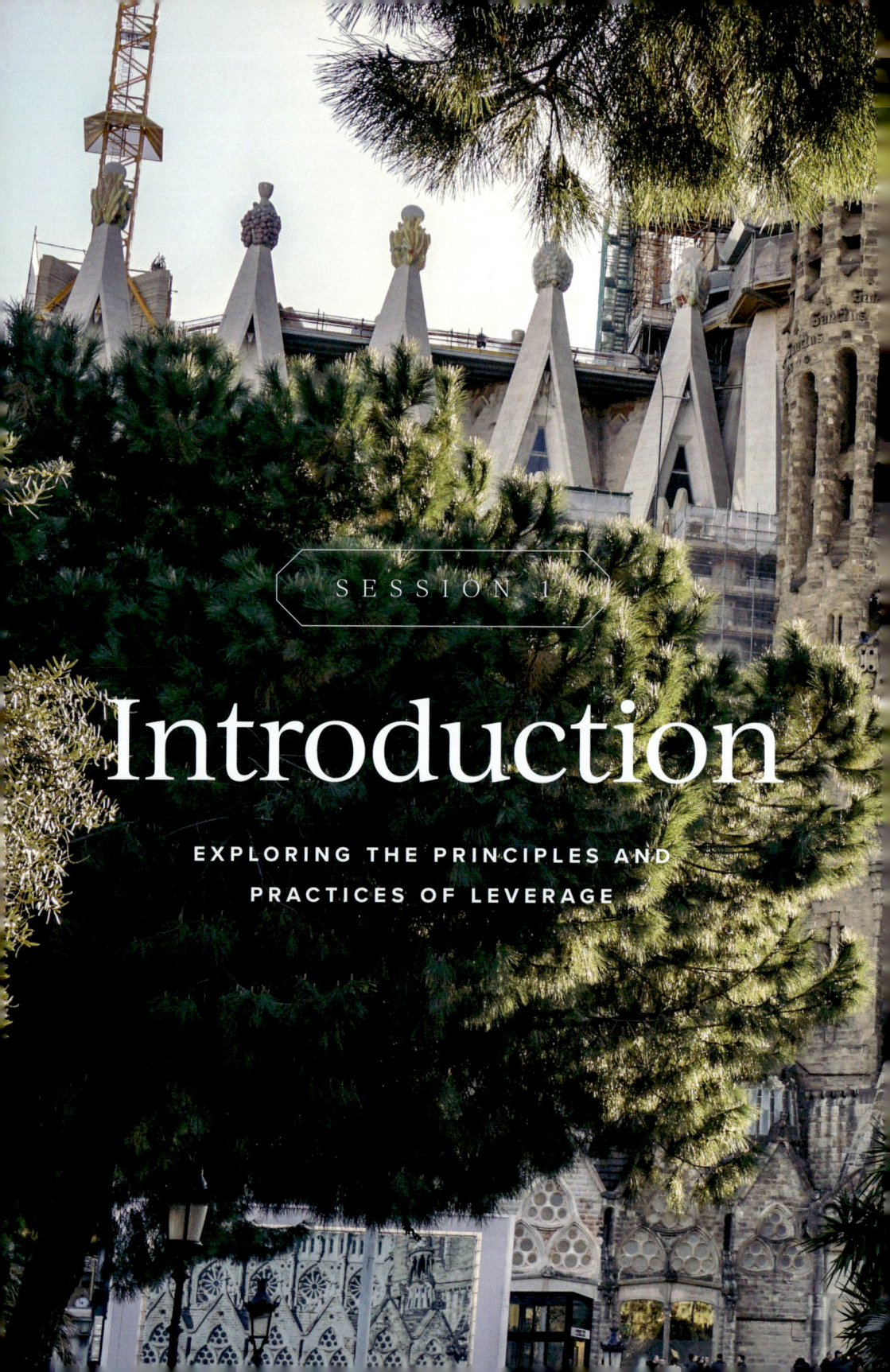

SESSION 1

Introduction

EXPLORING THE PRINCIPLES AND PRACTICES OF LEVERAGE

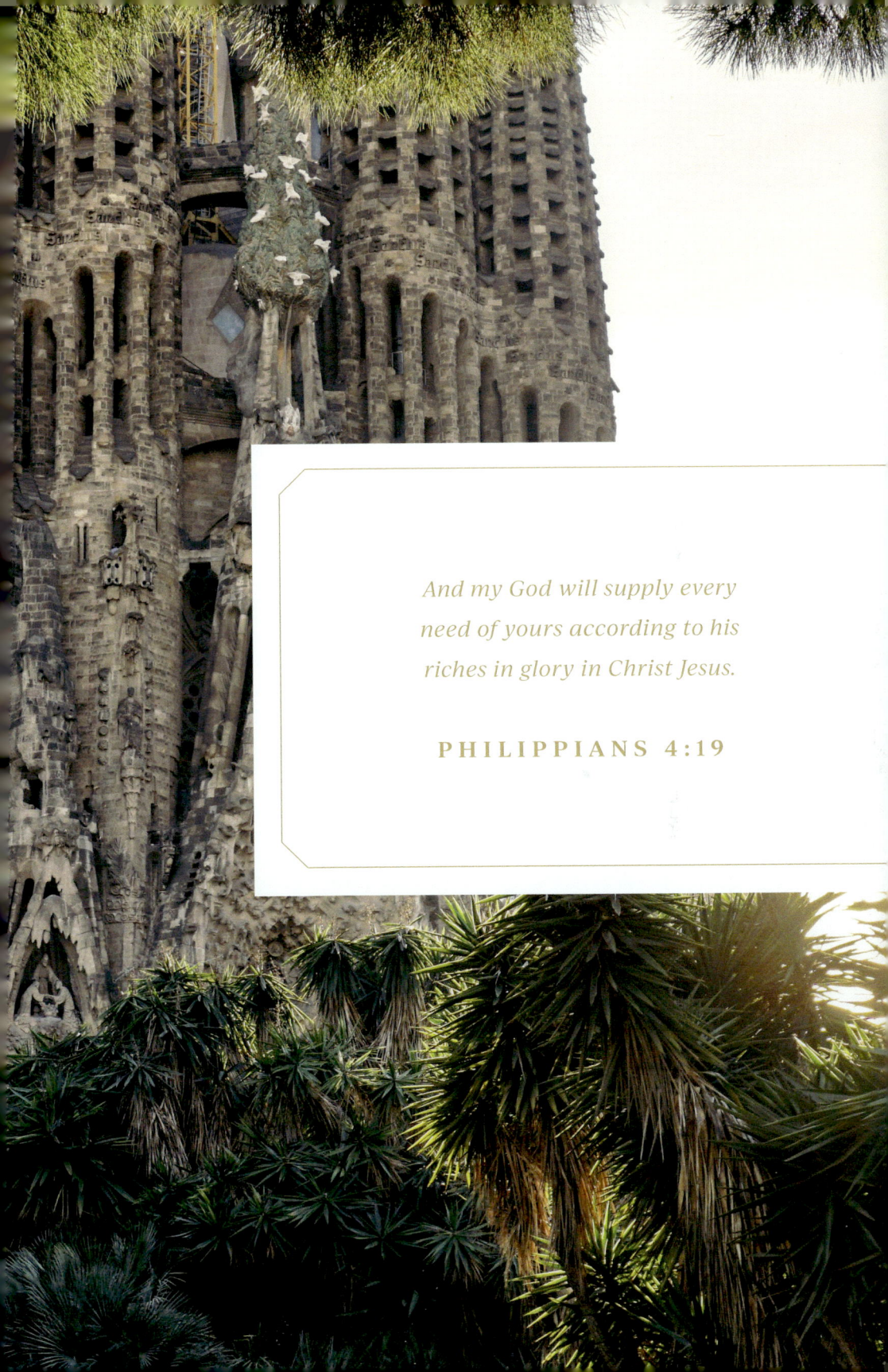

And my God will supply every need of yours according to his riches in glory in Christ Jesus.

PHILIPPIANS 4:19

INTRODUCTION

Open your group with prayer.

This prayer should be brief, simple, and invite God to be with each member as they meet. You can pray for specific requests at the end of the meeting, or stop momentarily to pray if a particular situation comes up during your discussion.

Before the first meeting starts, group members should ask for contact information from every participant so that you can connect between meetings. This step is voluntary, so there is no need to share your information with anyone if you wish not to do so.

Icebreaker

Begin this time together by using the following questions to get people talking:

- How has generosity been modeled for you?

- Who has modeled generosity for you?

VIDEO TEACHING

Watch the Video

Use the notes space below to record key thoughts, questions, and insights you want to remember or follow up on.

To watch, scan the QR code or go to: leverageyourlegacy.org/session1

Group Discussion

After watching the video, someone should read the discussion questions and direct the discussion among the group. As you go through each subsequent section, someone else should read the questions and direct the discussion.

1. Read 1 Timothy 6:17. How can riches be uncertain? What does God provide?

2. In the video Ken said, "God uses abundance to test us, to train us, to teach us, and to reveal faithfulness." How have you seen these tests play out in your life?

3. What did you think about the principle of limited sphere? (Russ spoke about this concept in the video.)

4. What kind of legacy do you want to leave?

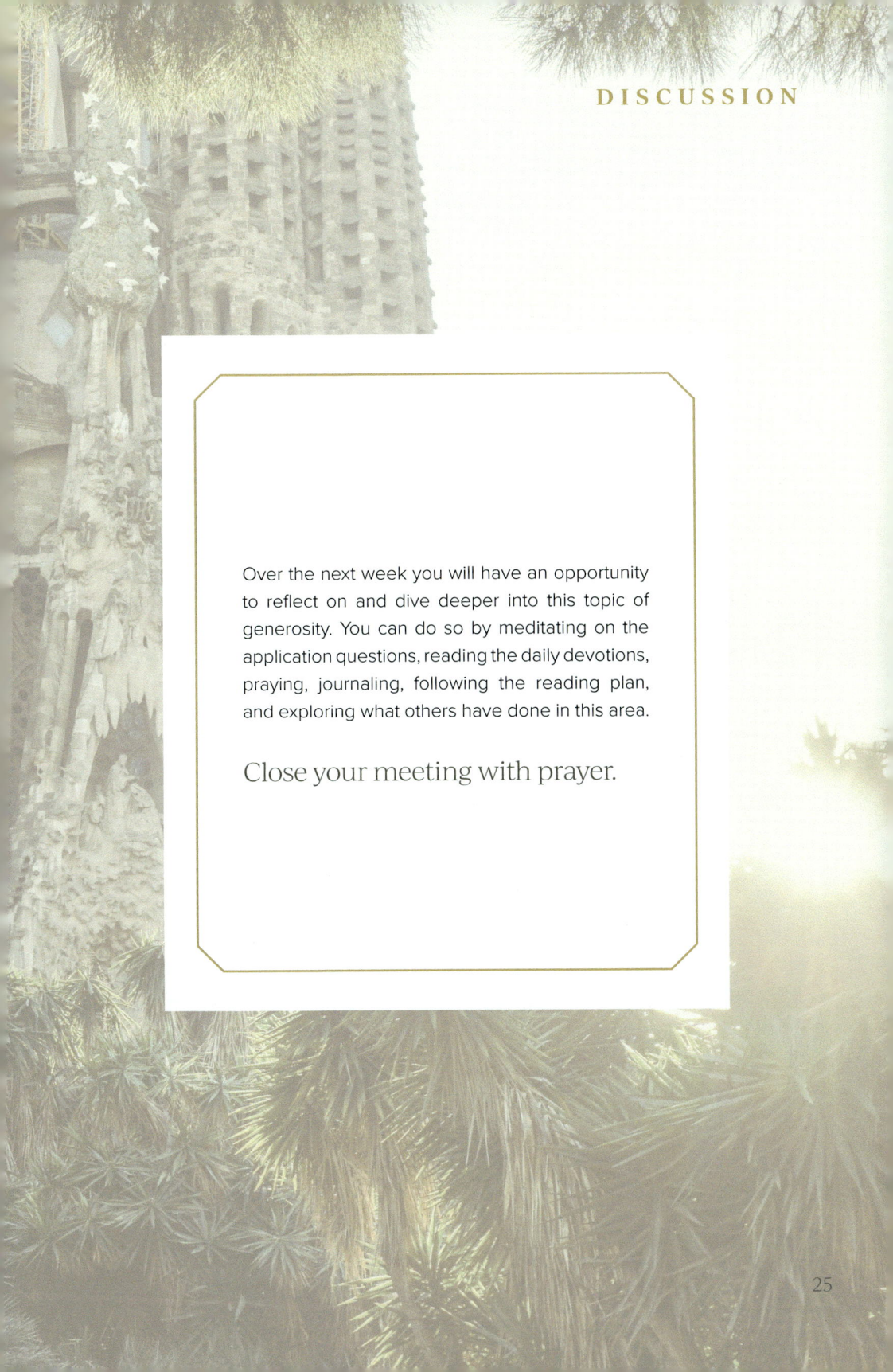

DISCUSSION

Over the next week you will have an opportunity to reflect on and dive deeper into this topic of generosity. You can do so by meditating on the application questions, reading the daily devotions, praying, journaling, following the reading plan, and exploring what others have done in this area.

Close your meeting with prayer.

25

Application

APPLICATION

1   Read Philippians 4:8. What do you tend to dwell on? How would dwelling on this list make a difference in your life?

2   Generally speaking, what does stewardship look like in the areas of time, talent, treasure, truth, and trust? Describe one area you are stronger in and one area you may struggle with?

3   Read Psalm 37:37 NASB. What is the difference between prosperity and posterity? What is one thing you can learn and might desire to live out in your life?

4   What is one step you can take to start moving or continue moving in your generosity journey?

Daily Devotions

DAY 1

Read James 1:5

"If any of you lacks wisdom, let him ask God, who gives generously to all without reproach, and it will be given him."

REFLECT

How can you demonstrate wisdom in your use of money?

_____
_____
_____
_____
_____
_____
_____
_____

DAY 2

Read Matthew 7:24-27

"Everyone then who hears these words of mine and does them will be like a wise man who built his house on the rock. And the rain fell, and the floods came, and the winds blew and beat on that house, but it did not fall, because it had been founded on the rock. And everyone who hears these words of mine and does not do them will be like a foolish man who built his house on the sand. And the rain fell, and the floods came, and the winds blew and beat against that house, and it fell, and great was the fall of it."

REFLECT

What are you building on? Rocks or sand?

_____
_____
_____
_____

DAILY DEVOTIONS

DAY 3

Read Proverbs 11:25

"Whoever brings blessing will be enriched, and one who waters will himself be watered."

REFLECT
How many people are you impacting now?

DAY 4

Read Psalm 37:4

"Delight yourself in the Lord, and he will give you the desires of your heart."

REFLECT
How can you put a cap on your desires?

DAILY DEVOTIONS

DAY 5

Read Matthew 6:3-4

"But when you give to the needy, do not let your left hand know what your right hand is doing, so that your giving may be in secret. And your Father who sees in secret will reward you."

REFLECT

How can you give in a way that calls attention to God and not to yourself?

DAY 6

Reflect

Reflect on the verses from this past week, and use the following space to write any thoughts God has put in your heart and mind from this session or during your Daily Devotions and Reading Plan.

Reading Plan

The *Leverage: Using Temporal Wealth for Eternal Gain* book is a great way to reinforce what you are learning in your small group time every week. The work you do on your own will greatly benefit you and your group time.

- ☐ **DAY 1:** Read pages 11-13.

- ☐ **DAY 2:** Explore generosity stories, best practices, and insights by scanning this QR Code or visit: **leverageyourlegacy.org/session1**

- ☐ **DAY 3:** Read pages 15-19.

- ☐ **DAY 4:** Explore generosity stories, best practices, and insights by scanning this QR Code or visit: **leverageyourlegacy.org/session1**

- ☐ **DAY 5:** Read pages 22-24.

- ☐ **DAY 6:** Reflect on the verses, devotions, and reading from this week.

EXPLORE

A Legacy of Giving Through the Generations

How much is too much to give? Peggy and Charles McCreight have come to understand that you can never out-give God. Throughout his career, Charles was blessed with financial success he didn't imagine he would receive. When the couple began experiencing this success, they met with a financial advisor who encouraged them to give.

The McCreights followed this advice, although it wasn't always easy or natural. Over the years, they have given much of their income away. Their financial giving has undoubtedly made a huge impact on organizations across the country, but Charles and Peggy also live out generosity in other ways. Just as important as their financial giving are the ways the couple gave away their time, expertise, and energy to hundreds of people. Through volunteer efforts around South Carolina and providing wise counsel to younger generations, they have influenced their circles as godly mentors.

The greatest blessing for the couple is that this habit of generosity continues to be a family value. Their grandchildren and even great-grandchildren show generosity through simple acts like lemonade stands to raise money for others. Generations of the McCreight family understand the joy of giving from the heart.

Read the Full Story

Scan the QR code to read the rest of the story and access other resources.

leverageyourlegacy.org/session1

SESSION 2

Why Are We to Give?

THE IMPORTANCE
OF ACCOUNTABILITY

The earth is the Lord's and the fullness thereof, the world and those who dwell therein,

PSALM 24:1

INTRODUCTION

Open your group with prayer.

This prayer should be brief, simple, and invite God to give you insight as you study. You can pray for specific requests at the end of the meeting, or stop momentarily to pray if a particular situation comes up during your discussion.

Check In

Ask, "Would anyone like to briefly share their thoughts about last week's session?"

Icebreaker

Begin this time together by using the following questions to get people talking:

- Looking at your own life, how has God provided for you in times of need?

- Have you experienced a spiritual reward in your heart and life through your generosity or the generosity of others? Tell the group about it.

VIDEO TEACHING

Watch the Video

Use the notes space below to record key thoughts, questions, and insights you want to remember or follow up on.

To watch, scan the QR code or visit: leverageyourlegacy.org/session2

Application

APPLICATION

1 | What are some practical ways in which you have been invited to participate in Kingdom work now?

2 | Looking at Ken's "Six Reasons for Giving," does a specific reason resonate with you? Why?

3 | Do you have peace of mind regarding your finances?

4 | Why do you think financial accountability is so hard to acquire and submit to?

5 | Do you have one person you can turn to who has the same values and world view as you? Come up with a name this week and tell the group at the next meeting. If you're ready, go ahead and set up time to meet with this person.

Daily Devotions

DAY 1

Read Matthew 6:19-21

"Do not lay up for yourselves treasures on earth, where moth and rust destroy and where thieves break in and steal, but lay up for yourselves treasures in heaven, where neither moth nor rust destroys and where thieves do not break in and steal. For where your treasure is, there your heart will be also."

REFLECT

What do your treasures say about the condition of your heart?

DAY 2

Read Luke 16:13

"No servant can serve two masters, for either he will hate the one and love the other, or he will be devoted to the one and despise the other. You cannot serve God and money."

REFLECT

Why is it impossible to serve both God and money? Who are you serving?

DAILY DEVOTIONS

DAY 3

Read John 10:10

"The thief comes only to steal and kill and destroy. I [Jesus] came that they may have life and have it abundantly."

REFLECT

Are you experiencing abundance or being robbed of it? What's draining abundance from your life?

DAY 4

Read 1 John 3:17

"But if anyone has the world's goods and sees his brother in need, yet closes his heart against him, how does God's love abide in him?"

REFLECT

What need are you aware of? How should you get involved?

DAILY DEVOTIONS

DAY 5

Read Revelation 22:12

Behold, I am coming soon, bringing my recompense with me, to repay each one for what he has done.

REFLECT
What kind of reward are you expecting from God?

DAY 6

Reflect

Reflect on the verses from this past week, and use the following space to write any thoughts God has put in your heart and mind from this session or during your Daily Devotions and Reading Plan.

Reading Plan

The *Leverage: Using Temporal Wealth for Eternal Gain* book is a great way to reinforce what you are learning in your small group time every week. The work you do on your own will greatly benefit you and your group time.

- ☐ **DAY 1:** Read pages 27-31 (stopping at the Six Reasons for Giving).

- ☐ **DAY 2:** Read pages 31-34.

- ☐ **DAY 3:** Read pages 34-36 & explore generosity stories, best practices, and insights by scanning this QR Code or going to: leverageyourlegacy.org/session2

- ☐ **DAY 4:** Read pages 85-89.

- ☐ **DAY 5:** Read pages 89-91 & explore generosity stories, best practices, and insights by scanning this QR Code or going to: leverageyourlegacy.org/session2

- ☐ **DAY 6:** Reflect on the verses, devotions, and reading from this week.

EXPLORE

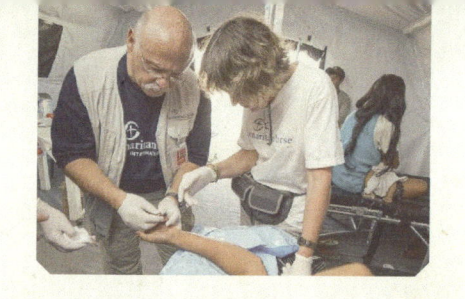

A Simple Stick of Chewing Gum

David Gettle, M.D., went into medicine because he wanted to help people. At medical school, he worked in a free clinic in inner-city Indianapolis. One day, an impoverished father of one of his patients had nothing to pay him but one stick of chewing gum, the only thing he could offer. Humbled by the generosity of this man, he was inspired for the rest of his life to do more.

In 1999, David was able to go into the medical mission field in Kosovo. "Needless to say, I had never worked in a war zone. But now I had to get an emergency room up and running in one, despite the fact there was only very sporadic electricity and precious few supplies. We even had to use batteries to run monitors and other medical equipment...It was truly an eye-opening experience."

In the most difficult places, from Kosovo to Iran and beyond, David learned that some of the most important things he could offer were compassion and God's love. He recalls the gratitude of a severely injured little girl's family when the volunteer team gave her a teddy bear in the midst of a horrific situation. "We were able to show compassion, which meant a lot to them."

> "Whatever you can do to help people in crisis or transition ...you'll receive blessings that you wouldn't have imagined."
>
> DAVID GETTLE, M.D.

David has delivered aid in the aftermath of many international crises, but he and his wife Karan note that you don't have to fly halfway around the world to help others in need. "Whatever you can do to help people in crisis or transition—well, all I can say is you'll receive blessings that you wouldn't have imagined," says David.

A Business Partnership with God

No one likes to give up control. Stanley Tam is no different. The only reason he relinquished the company he had started was because God was the one who was asking. As God increasingly blessed Stanley's business ventures with success, the amount of money available to donate also increased. In all, Stanley's business, U.S. Plastic Corporation, has given millions to God's work worldwide.

When Stanley began his first business venture, it failed. From that disappointment, he turned to God in prayer. He heard God say that Stanley would achieve business success if he turned the business over to Him. Stanley obeyed, and what God has done over the last almost century exceeded Stanley's wildest imagination. Along the way, Stanley responded with increasing obedience, eventually setting up a foundation to give 100% of the business's profits to Kingdom work.

God abundantly answered Stanley's prayers for business success, and in obedience, Stanley not only gave money away, but also gave his time. He spoke the Good News more than 7,000 times in 30 countries around the world.

Read the Full Story

Scan the QR code to read the rest of these stories and access other resources.

leverageyourlegacy.org/session2/

SESSION 3

When Are We to Give?

CURRENT VS. DEFERRED GIVING

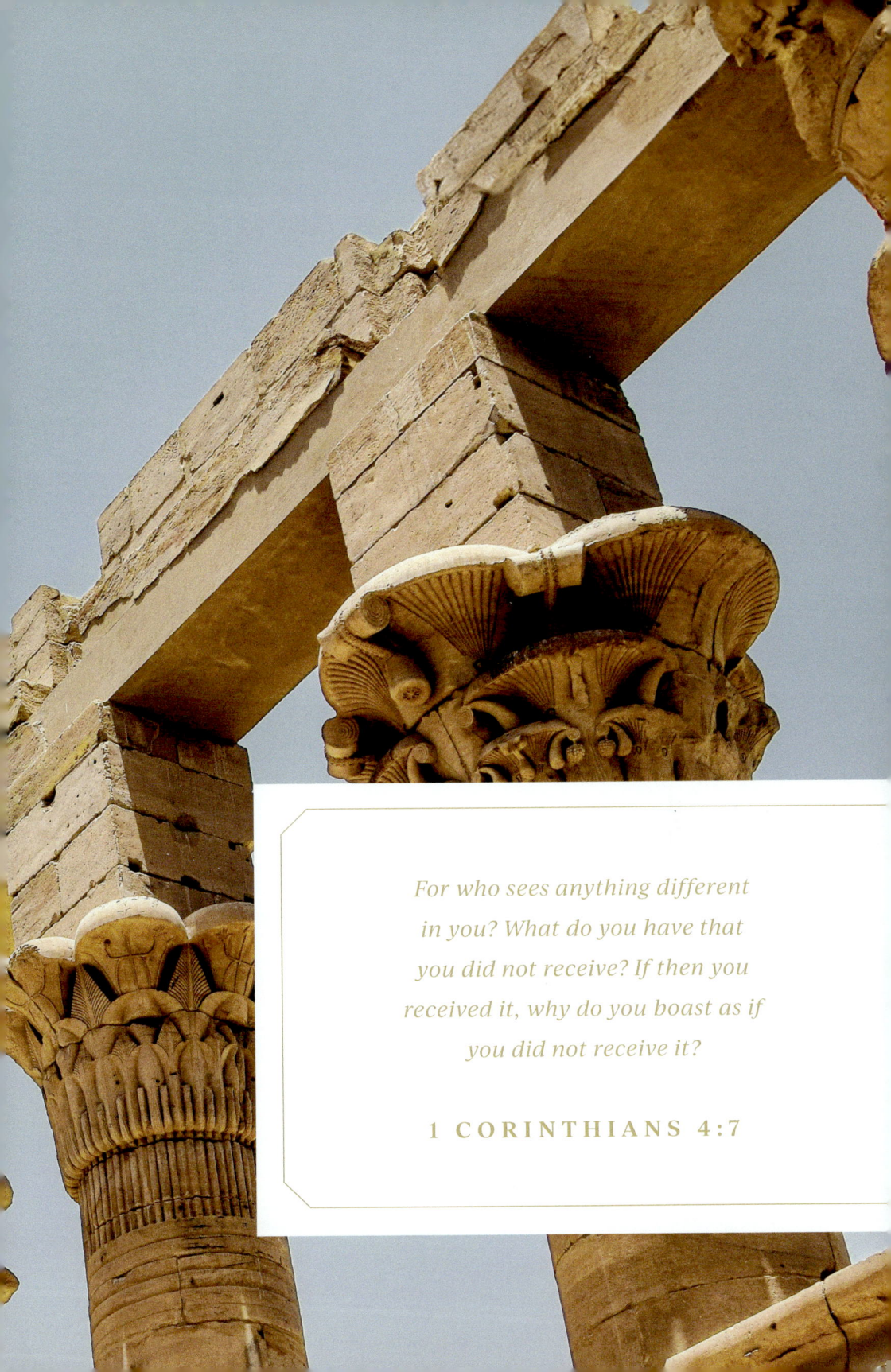

For who sees anything different in you? What do you have that you did not receive? If then you received it, why do you boast as if you did not receive it?

1 CORINTHIANS 4:7

INTRODUCTION

Open your group with prayer.

This prayer should be brief, simple, and invite God to be with you as you meet.

Check In

Ask, "Would anyone like to briefly share their thoughts about last week's session?"

Icebreaker

Begin this time together by using the following prompts to get people talking:

- Tell the group about a time you received an unexpected gift.

- At the end of the last session, you were asked to identify someone who you can turn to who has the same values and world view as you. Tell the group who you came up with.

VIDEO TEACHING

Watch the Video

Use the notes space below to record key thoughts, questions, and insights you want to remember or follow up on.

To watch, scan the QR code or go to: leverageyourlegacy.org/session3

Group Discussion

After watching the video, have someone read the questions below and direct the discussion among the group. As you go through each subsequent section, ask someone else to read the questions and direct the discussion.

1. What are your thoughts on the principle of reverse compounding discussed in the video? Have you ever thought of this concept?

2. Read Philippians 4:11-13. While most can imagine needing God's help in times of hunger and need, why do we need God's strength in times of abundance and plenty?

3. Read 2 Corinthians 8:2-4. What was the effect of affliction on the Corinthians' ability to give and to experience joy?

4. What did you think of Ken's comments in the video regarding the tithe in the old testament?

5. How can one leverage the currency of that which is passing away into the currency of that which will last forever?

6. Do you experience God as consistently abundant, or do you experience Him as withholding good gifts from your life? How does your giving reflect this mindset?

DISCUSSION

Over the next week you will have an opportunity to reflect on and dive deeper into this topic of generosity. You can do so by meditating on the application questions, reading the daily devotions, praying, journaling, following the reading plan, and exploring what others have done in this area.

Close your meeting with prayer.

Application

APPLICATION

1 | Share about a time you gave with an open hand. What was the result?

2 | Read Ephesians 1:3. How do you see God as the source of "every spiritual blessing" in your life?

3 | What are some ways you can participate with God in cultivating a Kingdom mindset of abundance and generosity, consistent with God's heart for His people? What's one thing you can start doing this week?

4 | What steps will you take this week to grow in your relationship with God? If you've focused on prayer in past weeks, maybe you'll want to direct your attention to Scripture this week. If you've been reading God's Word consistently, perhaps you'll want to take it deeper and try memorizing a verse. Tell the group which one you plan to try this week and talk about your progress and challenges when you meet next time.

Daily Devotions

DAY 1

Read Ephesians 2:4-7

"But God, being rich in mercy, because of the great love with which he loved us, even when we were dead in our trespasses, made us alive together with Christ—by grace you have been saved— and raised us up with him and seated us with him in the heavenly places in Christ Jesus, so that in the coming ages he might show the immeasurable riches of his grace in kindness toward us in Christ Jesus."

REFLECT

How does this passage demonstrate the transfer of earthly wealth to heavenly riches?

DAY 2

Read Psalm 36:7-8

"How precious is your steadfast love, O God! The children of mankind take refuge in the shadow of your wings. They feast on the abundance of your house, and you give them drink from the river of your delights."

REFLECT

How are you feasting on God's abundance?

DAILY DEVOTIONS

DAY 3

Read Leviticus 23:22

"And when you reap the harvest of your land, you shall not reap your field right up to its edge, nor shall you gather the gleanings after your harvest. You shall leave them for the poor and for the sojourner: I am the Lord your God."

REFLECT

How are you meeting the needs of others as God instructs us to do?

DAY 4

Read Romans 12:1

"I appeal to you therefore, brothers, by the mercies of God, to present your bodies as a living sacrifice, holy and acceptable to God, which is your spiritual worship."

REFLECT

How can you offer yourself as a sacrifice to God today?

DAILY DEVOTIONS

DAY 5

Read Hebrews 9:27

"And just as it is appointed for man to die once, and after that comes judgment,"

REFLECT

Although this thought seems bleak, how does this verse affect your thinking on generosity?

DAY 6

Reflect

Reflect on the verses from this past week, and use the following space to write any thoughts God has put in your heart and mind from this session or during your Daily Devotions and Reading Plan.

Reading Plan

The *Leverage: Using Temporal Wealth for Eternal Gain* book is a great way to reinforce what you are learning in your small group time every week. The work you do on your own will greatly benefit you and your group time.

- ☐ **DAY 1:** Read pages 37-41.

- ☐ **DAY 2:** Read pages 41-44.

- ☐ **DAY 3:** Read pages 44-47 & explore generosity stories, best practices, and insights by scanning this QR Code or going to: leverageyourlegacy.org/session3

- ☐ **DAY 4:** Read pages 93-99.

- ☐ **DAY 5:** Read pages 99-105 & explore generosity stories, best practices, and insights by scanning this QR Code or going to: leverageyourlegacy.org/session3

- ☐ **DAY 6:** Reflect on the verses, devotions, and reading from this week.

EXPLORE

It All Belongs to God

The de las Alases know what it is to have little and to have much. Both Gil and Jeane grew up in families who emigrated from the Philippines. Their parents worked hard and sometimes scraped to get by. When the couple had children, they made a tough but important decision that Jeane would stay home to raise their four children, making Gil the sole breadwinner.

Gil experienced much success in his human resources career, and the couple was blessed to be able to give away 15% of their income and strive for an even higher percentage. The importance of generosity is a legacy the family desires to instill in their children. They encourage them to set aside a portion of the money they earn to give to their Sunday school classes for God's work around the world.

The family also teaches their children the importance of giving not only financially but also with their time and talents. Whether it's through supporting international organizations or being a part of their church's mission work, the de las Alases are committed to the belief that all the gifts they have been given are owned by God and that we are called to hold them with an open hand.

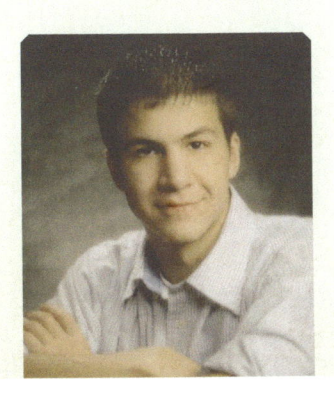

A God Jar, a Son's Heart, a Legacy

Brad Larson was only 22 when he was tragically killed in an automobile accident during his senior year at Taylor University. What his parents, Sherry and David Larson, discovered about their son after his death led them to think differently about what it means to have the heart of a giver.

In their growing-up years, the Larson children were encouraged to set aside 10% of the money they earned for savings and 10% for God. This lesson in accountability and generosity connected with Brad, and he was committed to it. As the Larsons looked through Brad's things after his death, they discovered a glass jar labeled with masking tape that said "God Jar." In the jar, Brad had set aside over $600 to give to God's work.

Along with this discovery, the Larsons were blessed with hundreds of letters from people whose lives Brad had impacted. One note described how meaningful it was when Brad gave a high school friend an envelope with $100 for her upcoming mission trip. The Larsons have been blessed by Brad's reflections and prayers found in his journals, and they compiled them into a book to provide encouragement to others.

Read the Full Story

Scan the QR code to read the rest of these stories and access other resources.

leverageyourlegacy.org/session3/

SESSION 4

How Are We to Give?

CASH FLOW VS.
NET WORTH GIVING

For you know the grace of our Lord Jesus Christ, that though he was rich, yet for your sake he became poor, so that you by his poverty might become rich.

2 CORINTHIANS 8:9

INTRODUCTION

Open your group with prayer.

This prayer should be brief, simple, and invite God to be with you as you meet.

Check In

Ask, "Would anyone like to briefly share their thoughts about last week's session?"

Icebreaker

Begin this time together by using the following question to get people talking:

- What are some common ways to give to ministries?

VIDEO TEACHING

Watch the Video

Use the notes space below to record key thoughts, questions, and insights you want to remember or follow up on.

To watch, scan the QR code or go to: <u>leverageyourlegacy.org/session4</u>

Group Discussion

After watching the video, have someone read the questions below and direct the discussion among the group. As you go through each subsequent section, ask someone else to read the questions and direct the discussion.

1. Read Matthew 6:1-4. What makes one a hypocritical giver? How do you avoid this trap?

2. Read 2 Corinthians 8:3. Are you giving according to your ability? How might looking at your assets affect your answer?

3. Read 1 Chronicles 29: 14-17. What's the benefit to public giving?

4. What were your thoughts on Russ' comments in the video regarding cash flow and net worth giving?

DISCUSSION

Over the next week you will have an opportunity to reflect on and go deeper into this topic of generosity. You can do so by meditating on the application questions, reading the daily devotions, praying, journaling, following the reading plan, and exploring what others have done in this area.

Close your meeting with prayer.

Application

APPLICATION

1 Have you ever considered giving an appreciated asset to charity? Why or why not?

2 What could you begin doing to implement giving from your assets or from your business?

3 Do you find yourself hesitant to give? Why or why not? If you are hesitant, what can you do to change this?

4 In what ways do you sense the Holy Spirit urging you to be generous? Be as specific as you can. What step can you take this week to expand your generosity?

Daily Devotions

DAY 1

Read 2 Corinthians 9:6

"The point is this: whoever sows sparingly will also reap sparingly, and whoever sows bountifully will also reap bountifully."

REFLECT

How is your sowing or giving proportionate to your means? What are you reaping?

_____
_____
_____
_____
_____
_____
_____
_____
_____
_____

DAY 2

Read James 1:17

"Every good gift and every perfect gift is from above, coming down from the Father of lights, with whom there is no variation or shadow due to change."

REFLECT

How is God blessing you these days?

_____
_____
_____
_____
_____
_____
_____
_____
_____
_____

DAILY DEVOTIONS

DAY 3

Read 2 Corinthians 2:15

"For we are the aroma of Christ to God among those who are being saved and among those who are perishing,"

REFLECT

What is your current level of influence among believers and non-believers? What can you do to increase your impact?

DAY 4

Read Philippians 4:15

"And you Philippians yourselves know that in the beginning of the gospel, when I left Macedonia, no church entered into partnership with me in giving and receiving, except you only."

REFLECT

What unique impact could you make today?

DAILY DEVOTIONS

DAY 5

Read 2 Corinthians 8:12-14

"For if the readiness is there, it is acceptable according to what a person has, not according to what he does not have. For I do not mean that others should be eased and you burdened, but that as a matter of fairness your abundance at the present time should supply their need, so that their abundance may supply your need, that there may be fairness."

REFLECT

What need could your abundance supply today?

_____
_____
_____
_____
_____
_____
_____
_____
_____

DAY 6

Reflect

Reflect on the verses from this past week, and use the following space to write any thoughts God has put in your heart and mind from this session or during your Daily Devotions and Reading Plan.

_____
_____
_____
_____
_____
_____
_____
_____
_____
_____
_____

Reading Plan

The *Leverage: Using Temporal Wealth for Eternal Gain* book is a great way to reinforce what you are learning in your small group time every week. The work you do on your own will greatly benefit you and your group time.

- [ ] **DAY 1:** Read pages 49-53.

- [ ] **DAY 2:** Read pages 53-58.

- [ ] **DAY 3:** Read pages 107-110 & explore generosity stories, best practices, and insights by scanning this QR Code or going to: leverageyourlegacy.org/session4

- [ ] **DAY 4:** Read pages 110-112.

- [ ] **DAY 5:** Read pages 112-114 & explore generosity stories, best practices, and insights by scanning this QR Code or going to: leverageyourlegacy.org/session4

- [ ] **DAY 6:** Reflect on the verses, devotions, and reading from this week.

EXPLORE

A Mission to Help Solve the Water Crisis

"Safe water for now and the 'Living Water' for eternity." This statement summarizes the mission that encouraged Molly and George Greene to provide clean water to those without it through their nonprofit organization, Water Mission. Their ministry provides sustainable, safe water solutions to people in developing countries or who are recovering from disasters.

Through compassion and a prompting from God to use the knowledge gained from twenty years of work with their environmental consulting company, George Greene designed a water treatment system to help in the aftermath of Hurricane Mitch, which hit Central America in 1998. This humble obedience uncovered a calling to help address the global water crisis, which eventually led to the creation of Water Mission.

As of 2024, Water Mission has completed over 3,200 projects in 60 countries and helped more than eight million people have access to clean water. Although the Greenes have learned much about water treatment systems since they first responded to God's tug on their hearts in 1998, they began with little knowledge of these systems but a desire to be obedient, serve others, and utilize their talents.

Read the Full Story

Scan the QR code to read the rest of these stories and access other resources.

leverageyourlegacy.org/session4/

Intentional Giving Ignited by the Difference Between a Decimal and a Comma

Kim King had felt God's nudge to increase her giving. As a successful corporate attorney, her focus had been on working. Her savings and giving were on autopilot, and when she felt convicted to look more closely at her finances after a Generous Giving event, Kim realized she was not actually as generous as she thought.

Striving to do better and with the best intentions, it took a punctuation oops for Kim to follow through on her self-proposed giving commitment. But in that moment, Kim felt God saying, "This is a journey, and I'm with you on it; it's going to be okay."

Soon after, Kim agreed to share her story at an event for Women Doing Well, which is an organization that seeks to inspire women toward purposeful generosity. Since then, Kim has spoken at numerous women's events and published a book on how women can lead generous lives. Kim keeps living out the lessons she teaches as she creates a giving plan each year and focuses on donating to organizations near her heart.

SESSION 5

How Much Are We to Give?

FINDING THE FINISH LINE

Each one must give as he has decided in his heart, not reluctantly or under compulsion, for God loves a cheerful giver.

2 CORINTHIANS 9:7

INTRODUCTION

Open your group with prayer.

This prayer should be brief, simple, and invite God to be with you as you meet.

Check In

Ask, "Would anyone like to briefly share their thoughts about last week's session?"

Icebreaker

Begin this time together by using the following question to get people talking:

- Who is the most generous person you know? What do you admire about them?

VIDEO TEACHING

Watch the Video

Use the notes space below to record key thoughts, questions, and insights you want to remember or follow up on.

To watch, scan the QR code or go to: leverageyourlegacy.org/session5

Group Discussion

After watching the video, have someone read the questions below and direct the discussion among the group. As you go through each subsequent section, ask someone else to read the questions and direct the discussion.

1. Read Luke 21:1-4. Why did Jesus praise the widow's gift? What would this kind of giving look like in your life?

2. Read Mark 10:21-22. Why do you think the rich man was disheartened by Jesus' request? Why did Jesus make this request of him?

3. Read 1 Timothy 6:8-10. How have you seen the principle in this verse played out in someone's life? How do you protect yourself from this outcome?

4. How do you ensure that you are giving according to your ability?

5. What would you do if you realized your net worth exceeded your finish line? Spend some time this week evaluating your finish line and imagining how you would generously invest the surplus of your net worth.

DISCUSSION

Individuals who are being filled up by God make a strong group and are empowered to love one another. What specific steps will you take this week to connect with God privately, so He can "fill you up?" If you've focused on prayer in past weeks, maybe you'll want to direct your attention to Scripture this week. If you've been reading God's Word consistently, perhaps you'll want to take it deeper and try memorizing a verse. Tell the group which one you plan to try this week. Then, at your next meeting, let everyone share about their progress and challenges.

Close your meeting with prayer.

Application

APPLICATION

1 | How much is enough, and how can you find that number?

2 | What causes are you passionate about, and do you wonder, "How much can I give?"

3 | What are your stumbling blocks to giving sacrificially?

4 | Read Mark 10:29-30. What is Jesus' promise regarding sacrificial giving?

5 | Pray for individuals you know who might respond to a simple invitation to come to a church service, join your small group, or even just have coffee and talk about spiritual matters. Ask the Holy Spirit to bring to mind people you can pray for.

Daily Devotions

DAY 1

Read Luke 9:23

"And [Jesus] said to all, 'If anyone would come after me, let him deny himself and take up his cross daily and follow me.'"

REFLECT

What does it mean for you to take up your cross daily and follow Jesus?

DAY 2

Read Ecclesiastes 5:10

"He who loves money will not be satisfied with money, nor he who loves wealth with his income; this also is vanity."

REFLECT

How satisfied are you? What are you using to try and satisfy yourself?

DAILY DEVOTIONS

DAY 3

Read Matthew 6:24

"No one can serve two masters, for either he will hate the one and love the other, or he will be devoted to the one and despise the other. You cannot serve God and money."

REFLECT
How are you experiencing this pull in your life?

DAY 4

Read Mark 10:25

"It is easier for a camel to go through the eye of a needle than for a rich person to enter the kingdom of God."

REFLECT
How much have you surrendered to God? What's holding you back?

DAILY DEVOTIONS

DAY 5

Read James 5:1-3

"Come now, you rich, weep and howl for the miseries that are coming upon you. Your riches have rotted and your garments are moth-eaten. Your gold and silver have corroded, and their corrosion will be evidence against you and will eat your flesh like fire. You have laid up treasure in the last days."

REFLECT

How is generosity an antidote to the hoarder's dilemma?

DAY 6

Reflect

Reflect on the verses from this past week, and use the following space to write any thoughts God has put in your heart and mind from this session or during your Daily Devotions and Reading Plan.

Reading Plan

The *Leverage: Using Temporal Wealth for Eternal Gain* book is a great way to reinforce what you are learning in your small group time every week. The work you do on your own will greatly benefit you and your group time.

- ☐ **DAY 1:** Read pages 59-62.

- ☐ **DAY 2:** Read pages 63-68.

- ☐ **DAY 3:** Read pages 68-70 & explore generosity stories, best practices, and insights by scanning this QR Code or going to: leverageyourlegacy.org/session5

- ☐ **DAY 4:** Read pages 115-120.

- ☐ **DAY 5:** Read pages 120-123 & explore generosity stories, best practices, and insights by scanning this QR Code or going to: leverageyourlegacy.org/session5

- ☐ **DAY 6:** Reflect on the verses, devotions, and reading from this week.

EXPLORE

Drawing a Line in the Sand

"Enough is never enough." Steve and Linda had this epiphany after meeting with their financial advisor. Steve was financially successful from an early age, which allowed the couple to live a very comfortable lifestyle. They thought they were set for a life of ease, only to discover how much they would need to continue earning to maintain that comfortable lifestyle.

After that financial planning meeting, Steve and Linda drew a line in the sand ("how much is enough") to determine their lifestyle limit, and they would give away everything above that. They stuck to their decision and giving plan despite the ups and downs that inevitably came their way. Over their many years of giving, Steve and Linda have intentionally looked for ways to be involved in the ministries they donate to on a regular basis.

> Steve and Linda drew a line in the sand ("how much is enough") to determine their lifestyle limit, and they would give away everything above that.

From caring for and founding a nonprofit that provides love and dignity to deceased newborn babies to a pastoral ministry in rural Ukraine, Steve and Linda have had their eyes opened to needs throughout the world and have stretched beyond their past giving to see how much more they can give. They also rejoice in the family legacy of generosity they have seen through their children.

We Haven't Been Able to Out Give God

"He just kept pouring more into us." This statement is how Monya Giles described God's blessing to her and her husband David. Although they started their marriage without a refrigerator or stove, God has blessed the couple abundantly. When David's business began to experience success, the couple became connected with Crown Financial Ministries and used its principles as guides to their financial future.

Even when David retired and began a hobby business, God blessed it by making it more successful than anything else he had done. The Giles continued to give generously and set up a donor-advised fund that brought the opportunity to involve their children in researching and choosing causes to support.

The Giles have experienced God's faithfulness time and time again. They are thankful for their humble beginnings, the valuable lessons they learned in those circumstances, and God's presence throughout. Now they have turned their attention to letting their children experience the importance and blessing of hard work.

Read the Full Story

Scan the QR code to read the rest of these stories and access other resources.

leverageyourlegacy.org/session5

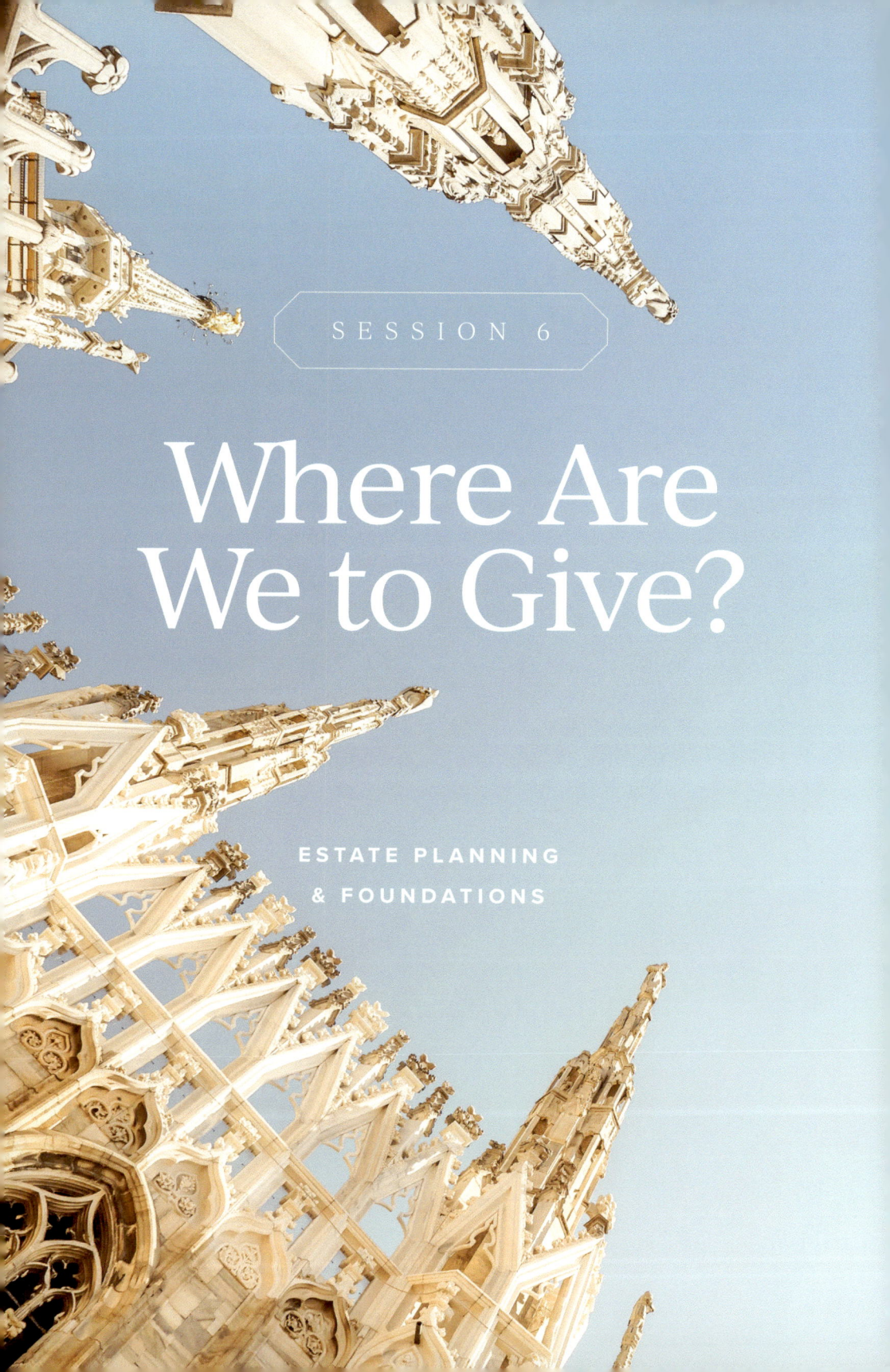

SESSION 6

Where Are We to Give?

ESTATE PLANNING
& FOUNDATIONS

*He must increase,
but I must decrease.*

JOHN 3:30

INTRODUCTION

Open your group with prayer.

This prayer should be brief, simple, and invite God to be with you as you meet.

Check In

Ask, "Would anyone like to briefly share their thoughts about last week's session?"

Icebreaker

Begin this time together by using the following question to get people talking:

- Last week you were left with the question, "What would you do if you realized your net worth exceeded your finish line?" What would you do?

VIDEO TEACHING

Watch the Video

Use the notes space below to record key thoughts, questions, and insights you want to remember or follow up on. **To watch, scan the QR code or go to:** leverageyourlegacy.org/session6

Application

APPLICATION

1   Have you made a plan for your current giving and your estate distributions? Why or why not? Do you have a current, up-to-date will?

2   Should a donor-advised fund or foundation be part of your estate plan? Should you be using a donor-advised fund or foundation now?

3   Write out a list of ministries you are currently connected to. Are there any that God might be calling you to participate with financially? Are there any names you should take off of your list?

4   When should you schedule a family meeting to intentionally communicate with your children about your estate plan?

Daily Devotions

DAY 1

Read Luke 12:15

"Take care, and be on your guard against all covetousness, for one's life does not consist in the abundance of his possessions."

REFLECT
What does your life consist of?

DAY 2

Read Galatians 6:6

"Let the one who is taught the word share all good things with the one who teaches."

REFLECT
As you read this verse, who comes to mind as a recipient of some of your giving?

DAILY DEVOTIONS

DAY 3

Read Matthew 10:16

"Behold, I am sending you out as sheep in the midst of wolves, so be wise as serpents and innocent as doves."

REFLECT
In what areas of your life could you use more wisdom?

DAY 4

Read Psalm 41:1

"Blessed is the one who considers the poor! In the day of trouble the Lord delivers him;"

REFLECT
Is some of your giving meeting the needs of the poor?

DAILY DEVOTIONS

DAY 5

Read James 2:14-16

"What good is it, my brothers, if someone says he has faith but does not have works? Can that faith save him? If a brother or sister is poorly clothed and lacking in daily food, and one of you says to them, "Go in peace, be warmed and filled," without giving them the things needed for the body, what good is that?"

REFLECT

How is your faith being expressed through your works and generosity?

_____
_____
_____
_____
_____
_____
_____
_____
_____

DAY 6

Reflect

Reflect on the verses from this past week, and use the following space to write any thoughts God has put in your heart and mind from this session or during your Daily Devotions and Reading Plan.

_____
_____
_____
_____
_____
_____
_____
_____
_____
_____
_____
_____

Reading Plan

The *Leverage: Using Temporal Wealth for Eternal Gain* book is a great way to reinforce what you are learning in your small group time every week. The work you do on your own will greatly benefit you and your group time.

- ☐ **DAY 1:** Read pages 71-74.

- ☐ **DAY 2:** Read pages 74-78.

- ☐ **DAY 3:** Read pages 125-128 & explore generosity stories, best practices, and insights by scanning this QR Code or going to: leverageyourlegacy.org/session6

- ☐ **DAY 4:** Read pages 128-132.

- ☐ **DAY 5:** Read pages 132-136 & explore generosity stories, best practices, and insights by scanning this QR Code or going to: leverageyourlegacy.org/session6

- ☐ **DAY 6:** Reflect on the verses, devotions, and reading from this week.

EXPLORE

A Move Out of Their Comfort Zone

Simply reading a book changed their lives—it wasn't just any book, and it wasn't just a small change. Steve and Marla Randolph read a book that challenges Christians to step out of their comfort zone, and it didn't take long for God to reveal how they should live out that calling.

A few years later, the Randolphs found themselves living in an urban area of Atlanta that looked and felt very different from their previous suburban home. Their new neighborhood is economically, culturally, and racially diverse but has an amazing sense of community. A church plant drew them to this location, and it is now the central point of their service.

In their new neighborhood, the Randolphs spend less time managing material things and driving to connect with people because they live in a home half the size of their previous one and can walk most places they need to go, which is not only convenient but also allows them to connect with their neighbors. This move has taught them the importance of not only giving financially, but also offering their time and energy to others. As a church elder, Steve has stepped into a shepherding role, and Marla is involved in discipling women. The Randolphs have embraced the philosophy of their new church: God has loved and served us well and calls us to love and serve our neighbors.

> This move has taught them the importance of not only giving financially, but also offering their time and energy to others.

Embracing a Dream: La Familia-Style

God opens doors, and we just need to walk through them. From a casual conversation at a family reunion to building a new orphanage in rural Mexico, Bill Lee embraces opportunities as God removes obstacles. He could never have imagined God's faithful provisions on this unexpected journey to save orphans.

As a successful businessman, Bill knew how to accomplish objectives and lead others. His corporate background helped him persevere through funding challenges and a language barrier to create a nonprofit organization committed to teaching orphans about the love of Jesus and providing them with an education so they can become financially independent adults.

Although there were obstacles along the way, Bill was instrumental in moving the orphanage to a different location where the new building doubles as a church and the children and community are part of each other. Bill remains in South Carolina for most of the year, but even there he has found ways to impact the Spanish community and leave a lasting impact.

Read the Full Story

Scan the QR code to read the rest of these stories and access other resources.

leverageyourlegacy.org/session6

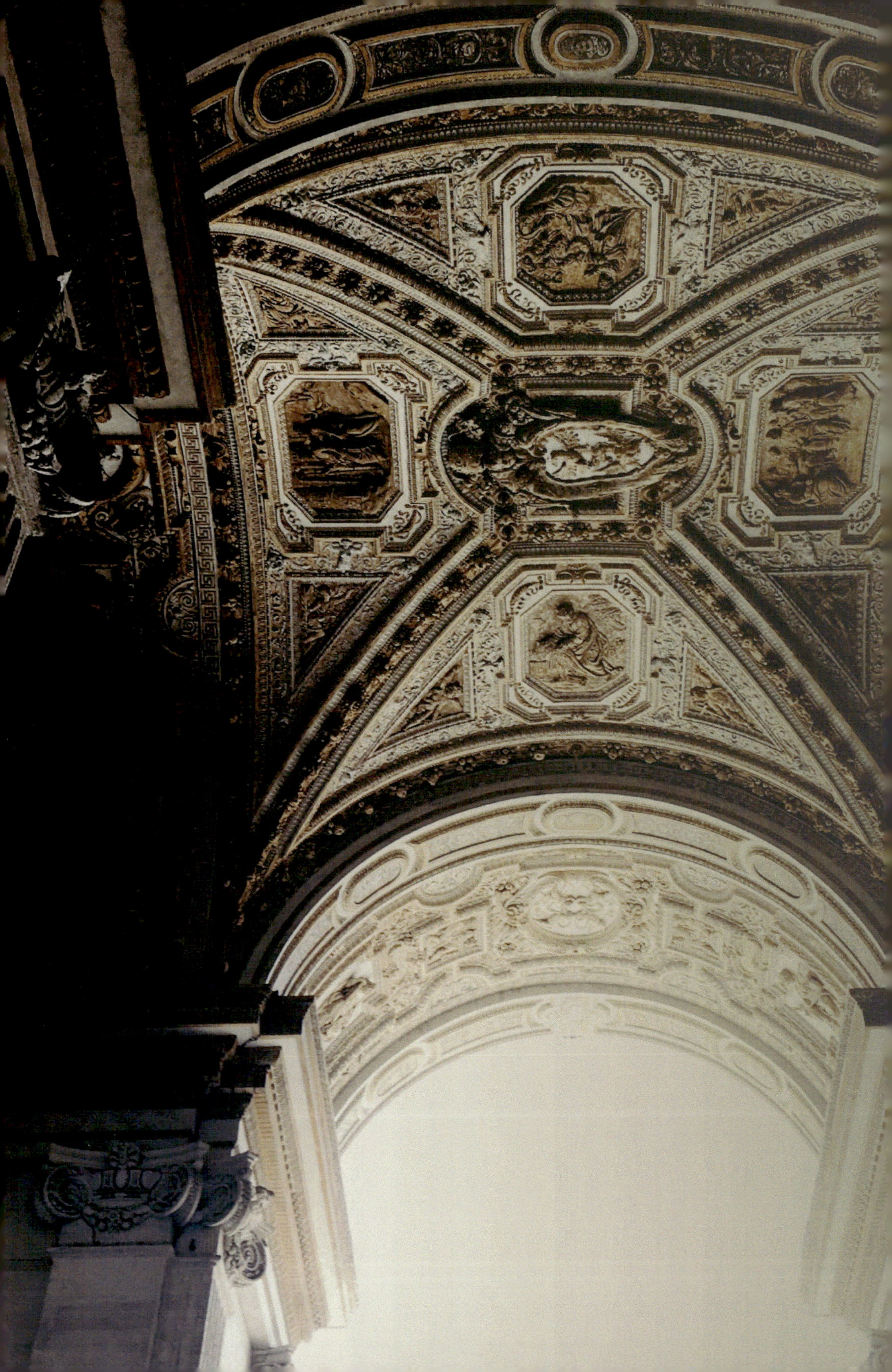

Appendices

Small Group Frequently Asked Questions

WHAT DO WE DO ON THE FIRST NIGHT OF OUR GROUP?

Like all fun things in life—have a party! A "get to know you" coffee, dinner, or dessert is a great way to launch a new study. You may want to review the Group Agreement on page 110 and share the names of a few friends you can invite to join you. But most importantly, have fun before your study time begins.

WHERE DO WE FIND NEW MEMBERS FOR OUR GROUP?

Forming a group can be difficult, especially if you are a new group with only a few people or an existing groups that has lost some people over time. We encourage you to pray with your group and then brainstorm a list of people from work, church, your neighborhood, your children's school, family, the gym, and so forth. Then have each group member invite several of the people on his or her list. Another good strategy is to ask church leaders to make an announcement or allow an insert in the welcome guide or bulletin.

No matter how you find members, it's vital that you stay on the lookout for new people to join your group. All groups tend to go through healthy attrition—the result of moves, releasing new leaders, ministry opportunities, etc.—and if the group gets too small, it could be at risk of shutting down. If you and your group stay open, you'll be amazed at the people God sends your way. The next person just might become a friend for life. You never know!

APPENDICES

HOW DO WE HELP GROUP MEMBERS FEEL COMFORTABLE?

Whether your group is new or ongoing, it's always important to reflect on and review your values together. On the next page is a Small Group Agreement with the values we've found most useful in sustaining healthy, balanced groups. We recommend that you choose one or two values—ones you haven't previously focused on or have room to grow in—to emphasize during this study. Choose values that will take your group to the next stage of intimacy and spiritual health.

If your group is new, welcome newcomers. Introduce everyone—you may even want to have name tags for your first meeting.

We recommend you rotate host homes on a regular basis and let the hosts lead the meeting. Studies show that healthy groups rotate leadership. This approach helps to develop every member's ability to shepherd a few people in a safe environment. Even Jesus gave others the opportunity to serve alongside Him (Mark 6:30-44). Review the following pages for additional information about hosting or leading the group.

The Small Group Calendar on page 112 is a tool for planning who will host and lead each meeting. Take a few minutes to plan hosts and leaders for your remaining meetings. Don't skip this important step! It will revolutionize your group. If anyone is hesitant, simply tell them to think about it, and you'll get back to them.

HOW LONG WILL THIS GROUP MEET?

Most groups meet weekly for at least their first six weeks, but every other week can work as well. We strongly recommend that the group meet weekly for the first six months if at all possible. This cadence allows for continuity, and if people miss a meeting, they aren't gone for an entire month.

At the end of this study, each group member may decide if he or she wants to stay for another study. Some groups launch relationships for years to come, and others are stepping-stones into another group experience. Either way, enjoy the journey!

CAN WE DO THIS STUDY ON OUR OWN?

Absolutely! This may sound crazy, but one of the best ways to do this study is not with a full house, but with a few friends. You may choose to gather with another couple who would enjoy some relational time (perhaps going to the movies or having a quiet dinner) and then walking through this study together. Jesus will be with you even if there are only two of you (Matthew 18:20).

WHAT IF THIS GROUP IS NOT WORKING FOR US?

You're not alone! This could be the result of a personality conflict, life stage difference, geographical distance, level of spiritual maturity, or any number of things. Relax. Pray for God's direction, and at the end of this six-week study, decide whether to continue with this group or find another. You don't typically buy the first car you look at or marry the first person you date, and the same goes with a group. However, don't quit before the study is over—God might have something to teach you. Also, don't run from conflict or prejudge people before you have given them a chance. God is still working in your life, too!

WHO IS THE LEADER?

Most groups have an official leader. But ideally, the group will mature and members will rotate the leadership of meetings. Healthy groups usually rotate hosts/leaders and homes on a regular basis. This model ensures that all members grow, give their unique contribution, and develop their gifts. This study guide and the Holy Spirit can keep things on track even when you rotate leaders. Christ has promised to be among you as you gather. Ultimately, God is your leader each step of the way.

HOW DO WE HANDLE THE CHILDCARE NEEDS IN OUR GROUP?

Very carefully. Seriously, this issue can be sensitive. We suggest that you empower the group to openly brainstorm solutions. You may try one option that works for a while and then adjust over time. One approach is for adults to meet in the living room or dining room and to share the cost of a babysitter (or two) who can watch the kids in a different part of the house. This way, parents don't have to be away from their children all evening when their children are too young to be left at home. A second option is to use one home for the kids and a second home (close by or a phone call away) for the adults. Another idea is to rotate the responsibility of providing a lesson or care for the children either in the same home or in another home nearby. This option can be an incredible blessing for kids. Finally, the most common solution is to decide that you need to have a night to invest in your spiritual lives individually or as a couple and to make your own arrangements for childcare. No matter what decision the group makes, the best approach is to dialogue openly if there is a struggle and try to help one another find a solution.

HOW DO WE HELP ONE ANOTHER SHARE THEIR GIFTS IN OUR GROUP?

Each member of a group has different gifts and abilities. Every small group has tasks and roles that need to be completed. How could you serve this group—perhaps with hospitality or prayer, by organizing an event, researching a topic, or inviting new people?

Spend some time praying about those you know who might respond to a simple invitation to come to a church service, join your small group, or just have coffee and talk about spiritual matters. Ask the Holy Spirit to bring to mind people you can pray for.

Groups grow closer when they serve together. How could your group serve someone in need? You may want to visit those who are homebound from your church, provide a meal for a family who is going through difficulty, or volunteer together at a local charity or ministry. If nothing comes to mind, spend time praying and asking God to show you who needs your help. Have two or three group members organize a serving project for the group, and then do it!

Small Group Agreement

OUR VALUES

Group Attendance	To give priority to the group meeting, we will call or email if we will be late or absent. (Completing the Group Calendar on the following pages will minimize this issue.)
Safe Environment	To help create a safe place where people can be heard and feel loved. (Please, no quick answers, snap judgments, or simple fixes.)
Respect Differences	To be gentle and gracious to fellow group members with different levels of spiritual maturity, personal opinions, temperaments, or "imperfections." We are all works in progress.
Confidentiality	To keep anything that is shared strictly confidential and within the group and to avoid sharing improper information about those outside the group.
Encourage Growth	To be not just takers but givers of life. We want to spiritually multiply our life by serving others with our God-given gifts.
Shared Ownership	To remember that every member is a minister and ensure that each attendee will share a small team role or responsibility over time.
Rotating Responsibilities	To encourage different people to host the group in their homes and rotate the responsibility of facilitating each meeting. (See the Group Calendar on page 112.)

APPENDICES

OUR PURPOSE

To provide a predictable environment where participants experience authentic community and spiritual growth.

OUR EXPECTATIONS

Refreshments/mealtimes _____
_____
_____
_____

Childcare _____
_____
_____
_____

When we will meet _____

We will begin at _____ and end at _____

Where we will meet (place) _____

We will do our best to have some or all of us attend a worship service together. Our primary worship service time will be _____.

Date of this agreement _____
Date we will review this agreement again _____

Who (other than the leader) will review this agreement at the end of this study?
_____

Small Group Calendar

DATE	LESSON	HOST HOME	DESSERT/MEAL	LEADER

APPENDICES

Small Group Roster

NAME	PHONE	EMAIL

Weekly Check-In

Briefly check in each week and write down your personal plans and progress targets for the next week (or even for the next few weeks). You can complete this check-in before or after the meeting, on the phone, through an email, or even in person from time to time.

	DATE	MY PLANS	MY PROGRESS
SESSION 1			
SESSION 2			
SESSION 3			
SESSION 4			
SESSION 5			
SESSION 6			

And my God will supply every need of yours according to his riches in glory in Christ Jesus.

PHILIPPIANS 4:19

The earth is the Lord's and the fullness thereof, the world and those who dwell therein.

PSALM 24:1

For who sees anything different in you? What do you have that you did not receive? If then you received it, why do you boast as if you did not receive it?

1 CORINTHIANS 4:7

For you know the grace of our Lord Jesus Christ, that though he was rich, yet for your sake he became poor, so that you by his poverty might become rich.

2 CORINTHIANS 8:9

Each one must give as he has decided in his heart, not reluctantly or under compulsion, for God loves a cheerful giver.

2 CORINTHIANS 9:7

He must increase, but I must decrease.

JOHN 3:30

APPENDICES

Prayer & Praise Report

	MY PLANS	MY PROGRESS
SESSION 1		
SESSION 2		
SESSION 3		
SESSION 4		
SESSION 5		
SESSION 6		

Small Group Leaders

KEY RESOURCES TO HELP YOUR LEADERSHIP EXPERIENCE BE THE BEST IT CAN BE.

Hosting an Open House

If you're starting a new group, try planning an "open house" before your first formal group meeting. Even if you have only two to four core members, it's a great way to break the ice and consider prayerfully who else might be open to joining you over the next few weeks. You can also use this kick-off meeting to hand out study guides, spend some time getting to know each other, discuss each person's expectations for the group, and briefly pray for each other. A simple meal or good desserts always make a kick-off meeting more fun.

After people introduce themselves and share how they ended up at the meeting (you can play a game to see who has the wildest story!), have everyone respond to a few icebreaker questions:

- What is your favorite family vacation?
- What is one thing you love about your church/our community?
- What are three things about your life growing up that most people here don't know?

Next, ask everyone to tell what he or she hopes to get out of the study. You might want to review the Small Group Agreement and talk about each person's expectations and priorities.

Finally, set an open chair (maybe two) in the center of your group and explain that it represents someone who would enjoy or benefit from this group but who isn't here yet. Ask people to pray about inviting someone to join the group over the next few weeks. Hand out postcards and have everyone write an invitation or two. Don't worry about ending up with too many people; you can always have one discussion circle in the living room and another in the dining room after you watch the lesson. Each group could then report prayer requests and progress at the end of the session.

You can skip this kick-off meeting if your time is limited, but you'll experience a huge benefit if you take the time to connect with each other in this way.

Leading for the First Time

- **Sweaty palms are a healthy sign.** The Bible says God is gracious to the humble. Remember who is in control; the time to worry is when you're not worried. Those who are soft in heart (and sweaty-palmed) are those whom God is sure to speak through.

- **Seek support.** Ask your leader, co-leader, or close friend to pray for you and prepare with you before the session. Walking through the study beforehand will help you anticipate potentially difficult questions and discussion topics.

- **Bring your uniqueness to the study.** Lean into who you are and how God wants you to uniquely lead the study.

- **Prepare. Prepare. Prepare.** Go through the session several times. If you are using the video session, listen to the teaching segment and Leadership Lifter. Consider writing in a journal or fasting for a day to prepare yourself for what God wants to do. Don't wait until the last minute to prepare.

- **Ask for feedback.** Perhaps in an email or on cards handed out at the study, have everyone write down three things that went well and one thing that could be improved on. Don't get defensive. Instead, show an openness to learn and grow.

- **Prayerfully consider launching a new group.** This doesn't need to happen overnight, but God's heart is for this to take place over time. Not all Christians are called to be leaders or teachers, but we are all called to be shepherds of a few someday.

- **Share with your group what God is doing in your heart.** God is searching for those whose hearts are fully His. Share your trials and victories. We promise that people will relate.

- **Prayerfully consider who you would like to pass the baton to the next week.** It's only fair. God is ready for the next member of your group to go on the faith journey you just traveled. Make it fun, and expect God to do the rest.

Leadership Training 101

CONGRATULATIONS! You have responded to the call to help shepherd Jesus' flock. There are few other tasks in the family of God that surpass the contribution you will be making. As you prepare to lead, whether it is one session or the entire series, here are a few thoughts to keep in mind. We encourage you to read these and review them with each new discussion leader before he or she leads.

1. **Remember that you are not alone.** God knows everything about you, and He knew that you would be asked to lead your group. Remember that it is common for all good leaders to feel that they are not ready to lead. Moses, Solomon, Jeremiah, and Timothy were all reluctant to lead. God promises, "...to never leave you nor forsake you" (Hebrews 13:5). Whether you are leading for one evening, for several weeks, or for a lifetime, you will be blessed as you serve.

2. **Don't try to do it alone.** Pray right now for God to help you build a healthy leadership culture. If you can enlist a co-leader to help you lead the group, your experience will be much richer. This is your chance to involve as many people as you can in building a healthy group. All you have to do is call and ask people to help. You'll probably be surprised at the response.

3. **Just be yourself.** If you won't be you, who will? God wants you to use your unique gifts and temperament. Don't try to do things exactly like another leader; do them in a way that fits you! Just admit it when you don't have an answer, and apologize when you make a mistake. Your group will love you for it, and you'll sleep better at night!

4. **Prepare for your meeting ahead of time.** Review the session and the leader's notes, and write down your responses to each question. Pay special attention to exercises that ask group members to do something other than engage in discussion. These exercises will help your group live what the Bible teaches, not just talk about it. Be sure you understand how an exercise works, and bring any necessary supplies (such as paper and pens) to your meeting. If the exercise employs one of the items, be sure to look over that item so you'll know how it works.

5. **Pray for your group members by name.** Before you begin your session, go around the room in your mind and pray for each member by name. You may want to review the prayer list at least once a week. Ask God to use your time together to touch the heart of every person uniquely. Expect God to lead you to whomever He wants you to encourage or challenge in a special way. If you listen, God will surely lead!

6. **When you ask a question, be patient.** Someone will eventually respond. Sometimes, people need a moment or two of silence to think about the question. Keep in mind, if silence doesn't bother you, it won't bother anyone else. After someone responds, affirm the response with a simple "thanks" or "good job." Then ask, "How about somebody else?" or "Would someone who hasn't shared like to add anything?" Be sensitive to new people or reluctant members who aren't ready to speak aloud, pray, or offer anything. If you give them a safe setting, they will blossom over time.

7. **Provide transitions between questions**. When guiding the discussion, always read aloud the transitional paragraphs and the questions. Ask the group if anyone would like to read the paragraph or Bible passage. Don't call on anyone, but ask for a volunteer, and then be patient until someone begins. Be sure to thank the person who reads aloud.

8. **Break up into smaller groups each week or they won't stay.** If your group has more than seven people, we strongly encourage you to have the group gather sometimes in discussion circles of three or four

people during the Discussion and Application sections of the study. With a greater opportunity to talk in a small circle, people will connect more with the study, apply more quickly what they're learning, and ultimately get more out of it.

A small circle can encourage a quiet person to participate and tends to minimize the effects of a more vocal or dominant member. It can also help people feel more loved in your group. Small circles are helpful during prayer time because people who are unaccustomed to praying aloud will feel more comfortable trying it with just two or three others. Also, prayer requests won't take as long in smaller groups, so circles will have more time to actually pray. When you gather back with the whole group, you can have one person from each circle briefly update everyone on the prayer requests. People are more willing to share in small circles if they know that the whole group will hear all the prayer requests.

9. **Rotate facilitators weekly.** At the end of each meeting, ask the group who should lead the following week. Let the group help select your weekly facilitator. You may be perfectly capable of leading each time, but you will help others grow in their faith and gifts if you give them opportunities to lead. You can use the Small Group Calendar to fill in the names of all meeting leaders at once if you prefer.

10. **One final challenge (for new or first-time leaders):** Before your first opportunity to lead, look up each of the five passages listed below. Read each one as a devotional exercise to help yourself develop a shepherd's heart. Trust us on this one. If you do this, you will be more than ready for your first meeting.

    - Matthew 9:36
    - 1 Peter 5:2-4
    - Psalm 23
    - Ezekiel 34:11-16
    - 1 Thessalonians 2:7-8, 11-12

Acknowledgments

We are so grateful to the individuals and organizations whose contributions made the *Leverage Study Guide* curriculum possible.

We also give thanks for the support and contribution of many at Blue Trust and Reflections Ministries who made this production possible. As Blue Trust's CEO, Brian Shepler provided us a platform to allow this project to come together for which we are eternally grateful. The content in the curriculum would not have been possible without the many decades of learnings from the many partners at Blue Trust. As the project gained momentum, Sandy Morgan and her capable Blue Trust team (Malissa Light, Brittany Allen, Perry Daniels, Wes Morgan, and Stefanie Painter) took up the baton and made sure the multitude of details were completed, including organizing and coordinating the filming of the town hall meeting, which came together without a hitch. We want to also give thanks to the Reflections Ministries' associates, Renee Wood and Michael Hitchcock, and Peter Boedy at Trinity House Publishers, for their assistance and support in this project.

In addition, we are very appreciative of First Redeemer Church in Cumming, GA for allowing us to use their wonderful space for our town hall filming. Many thanks to Associate Pastor Mike Schmidt for his partnership and support and for offering to help whenever we needed anything. It was a true blessing to film on their beautiful campus.

We are deeply thankful for the many friends, clients, and other associates who gave of their time to make the town hall audience come to life, shared as a panelist during the filming, or provided testimonies. Crawford Loritts, Brian Shepler, Anehita Chie, Claiborne Haw, Reed Crosson, and Evan Longstreth all added significant depth and insights to the curriculum as panelists. Bill and Alison Ibsen, Kenny Hill, John and Teri Hall, Marshall and Janice Potter, Barb and Dave Emrich, John and Jessica Gibson, Erik Daniels, John Fillinger, Crawford Loritts, Evan Longstreth, and Claiborne Haw provided eloquent testimonies that make this curriculum compelling and approachable.

As we launch this curriculum, we eagerly anticipate its impact on individuals seeking to understand and apply God's teachings on generosity and wealth. We are grateful for the continued support and engagement of our community as we journey together to discover God's timeless principles for eternal gain.

Next Steps

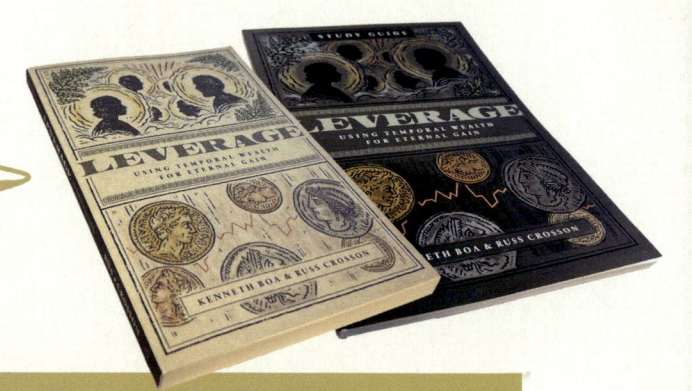

START A
LEVERAGE YOUR LEGACY
Small Group

Leverage Your Legacy Curriculum is Made For:

- Pastors and Church Leaders looking to teach biblical principles of stewardship and generosity to families of wealth.
- Christian Financial Advisors seeking a faith-based resource for their clients.
- Ministries and Organizations working with families of wealth, helping them align their financial practices with their faith.

Resources and Support

Access a wealth of additional resources online.

- Access a wealth of additional resources online.
- Leadership training sessions
- Small group hosting tips
- Video guides featuring Leverage authors Russ Crosson and Ken Boa
- Full access to planning and promotional tools for your church

SCAN QR CODE or go to leverageyourlegacy.org

BLUE TRUST

BlueTrust

If you have been challenged by this course, a good next step would be to contact Blue Trust. They have over 45 years of experience in helping people navigate their generosity journey. Blue Trust advisors apply biblical wisdom and technical expertise to help clients make wise financial decisions to experience clarity and confidence and leave a lasting legacy. They offer comprehensive financial services and objective advice to clients across the wealth spectrum in all 50 states. Their services include:

- Financial, retirement, and estate planning
- Investment management
- Cash flow and budget planning
- Charitable giving strategies
- Personal trust and estate settlement
- Business consulting services
- Family office
- Sports and entertainment services
- Institutional services
- Retirement plan consulting

For more information:

Contact Blue Trust by calling 888-709-7146, sending an email to **leverage@bluetrust.com**, or visiting their website at bluetrust.com.

GENEROUS GIVING

GENEROUSGIVING

Founded in 2000 by The Maclellan Foundation, Generous Giving is dedicated to fostering a culture of biblical generosity. Through open, donation-free conversations about God and money, we inspire followers of Christ to embrace a spirit-led commitment to giving. Our goal is to shift the focus from personal accumulation to a life marked by extravagant generosity.

Generous Giving envisions a transformative movement where Christians are recognized for their radical giving rather than consumption. We aim to create a shift in culture where generosity becomes a defining trait, drawing others to explore the God who inspires such giving. This movement is designed to deepen individuals' relationships with God, providing greater joy, freedom, and purpose as they trade earthly accumulation for eternal treasure.

Our efforts seek to release billions of dollars for God's Kingdom, advancing the gospel, serving those in need, and contributing to the healing of the world. By promoting a life of open-handed living, Generous Giving aims to make a significant impact both in individual lives and across global communities.

For more information: generousgiving.org

REFLECTIONS MINISTRIES

Reflections Ministries, established in 1995, builds upon Ken Boa's unique and extensive teaching resources, which began in 1983. These extensive resources on offer from the ministry include Dr. Boa's numerous books and publications, Dr. Boa's in-depth weekly study groups, the Reflections Ministries YouTube channel, curriculum and training materials, and the weekly Explorers Podcast. This ministry focuses on relational evangelism and discipleship, guiding individuals to know Christ, follow Him, and embody His life in their own.

The ministry is structured around three key pillars:

- **Loving Well:** This pillar emphasizes developing a deep, relational connection with God and others, based on the greatest commandments from Matthew 22:37-39. It involves pursuing spiritual excellence and fostering a heartfelt commitment to loving Christ above all else. In terms of imagery, this pillar emphasizes the centrality of the heart in one's devotion to Christ.

- **Learning Well:** This pillar is about intellectual and spiritual growth, encouraging thoughtful reflection on what is true, honorable, and commendable as outlined in Philippians 4:8. It aims to cultivate a mind that seeks and values wisdom and understanding. The image that corresponds to this pillar would be the head, symbolizing the life of the mind.

- **Living Well:** This pillar focuses on the practical application of love and learning in daily life. It includes managing time and resources wisely and embodying the principles of prayer and excellence found in Philippians 4:6-9. The goal is to translate spiritual insights into actionable, everyday practices. The image that corresponds to this pillar would be that of the hands, a fitting picture for care and servanthood.

Through these pillars, Reflections Ministries seeks to support a holistic journey of faith, helping individuals grow spiritually, intellectually, and practically in their walk with Christ.

For more information: **kenboa.org**

LIFETOGETHER

Lifetogether Ministries has been dedicated to transforming lives through community for over 25 years. Specializing in Christian media production and publishing, Lifetogether partners with churches and ministries to strategize, produce, and coach pastors/leaders, helping them leverage their life, leadership and legacy to inspire deeper connections within their congregations and communities.

Throughout its journey, Lifetogether has collaborated with respected leaders like Rick Warren, Max Lucado and John Maxwell, alongside thousands of pastors and best-selling authors, to create impactful video teachings and print curriculums that foster lasting spiritual growth in communities.

ALSO AVAILABLE FROM LIFETOGETHER:

- Additional training on launching and leading a Leverage ministry or a Leverage small group in your church, home, work or anywhere you can gather with friends, family or your clients.

- Receive a free 100-page digital workbook on how to start and sustain a Leverage small group. Title: *Doing Groups Together*.

- See additional case studies, testimonials, tools and resources from other growing churches launching Leverage in their church.

- Small group series and individual sessions from some of your favorite pastors, teachers and Christian leaders such as David Jeremiah, Christine Caine, Chris Hodges, Craig Groeschel, Greg Surratt, Randy Alcorn and more.

- Dozens of additional Next Step curriculum:
  - 40 Day Generosity campaigns and companion curriculum
  - Church-wide alignment campaigns
  - Resources to enlarge the heart of generosity in your church

For more information: lifetogether.com

FAMILY LEGACY PRODUCTIONS

Family Legacy Productions
PRESENTED BY LIFETOGETHER

Our team at LifeTogether is pleased to introduce you to **Family Legacy Productions,** your ultimate destination for producing and preserving your family's story, values, wisdom and even generosity. In today's fast-paced world, we recognize that despite the powerful bonds that connect families, the opportunity to pass down knowledge and cherished traditions can be limited. Our mission is to bridge generational gaps and empower your family's legacy and generosity through the very technology that sometimes separates us.

Family Legacy Productions are hosted (or co-hosted) by our team and provide the best of the skills of a wedding planner, film producer, family counselor, and camp director. We create an immersive legacy-capturing experience for families of any size.

- Personal interviews: (conducted for individuals, pairs, spouses, parent/child, generations, women/men, next generation kids, youngest, oldest, and just about any combination, etc.)
- Small Group panel/roundtable discussions (wide variety of topics, questions, groupings, settings, productions, etc.)
- Large group town-hall productions (two-way questions and answers)
- LEVERAGE MasterClass productions (mission, vision and values as well as dozens of other topics)
- Co-host LEVERAGE online gatherings (all together, generational, gender only, special committees, topical teams)

For more information: leverageyourlegacy.org/productions

MORE BY BLUE TRUST

Faces of Generosity

INSPIRING STORIES OF PEOPLE IMPACTING LIVES AROUND THE WORLD

From a widow in Florida who packs countless shoeboxes for Operation Christmas Child, to a dentist in California who designed a portable dental chair and equipment in order to treat people in the jungles of Brazil, to the couple in Georgia who moved to the heart of urban Atlanta in order to redefine community, to the North Carolina couple who adopted 15 children and never looked back.

The 27 stories in *Faces of Generosity* are true and inspiring stories of people who have followed God's calling (or sometimes nudging) to sacrificially help others. None of these Blue Trust clients were seeking fame or notoriety but all wanted to help others and make a difference in someone's life. Each had a unique story to tell and we're honored that they shared their stories with us.

For more information: bluetrust.com/generosity

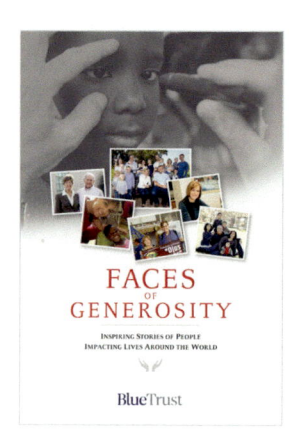

Email leverage@bluetrust.com to receive a complimentary copy of *Faces of Generosity*.

MORE BY RON BLUE

Ron Blue

FOUNDER OF RON BLUE INSTITUTE & BLUE TRUST

Founder of the Ron Blue Institute, Co-founder of Blue Trust (formerly Ronald Blue & Company), Kingdom Advisors, and the National Christian Foundation, Ron Blue has dedicated his career to helping Christians manage wealth for eternal impact.

Through his leadership, Blue Trust grew to advise on over $59 billion in assets for more than 10,000 clients across 17 offices nationwide, setting a standard for biblically grounded financial guidance. His ministry, Kingdom Advisors (KA), equips Christian financial professionals to apply biblical wisdom in their client advice, while the National Christian Foundation (NCF) helps generous families establish giving strategies that empower faithful and transformative stewardship.

Ron Blue's commitment to Kingdom-focused financial wisdom has led him to author more than 20 books on biblical personal finance, guiding Christians across the world toward wise stewardship and purposeful living.

In God Owns It All, Ron Blue explores the essential truths of financial stewardship rooted in Scripture. In the wealthiest nation in history, where even those at the poverty line are wealthier than 85% of the world, why do so many feel discontent? Ron's answer lies in biblical principles that reshape our understanding of wealth and lead to lives of purpose and contentment.

Unlock the freedom and fulfillment of biblical financial stewardship—because truly, God Owns It All.

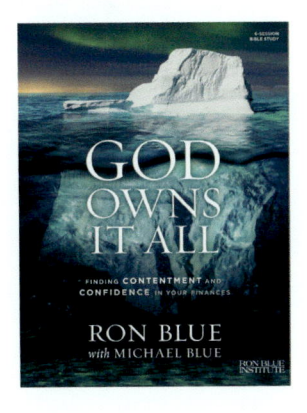

For more information: ronblueinstitute.com

MORE BY RUSS CROSSON

Your Life...Well Spent

THE ETERNAL REWARDS OF INVESTING YOURSELF AND YOUR MONEY IN YOUR FAMILY

When you think about money, you probably think about what it can do for you here, now, in this life. But did you know how you invest your money has an eternal impact?

Russ Crosson, author of *Your Life...Well Spent*, offers a unique look at how to manage your money with eternity in view. In this book, you'll learn the difference between prosperity—the accumulation of goods on this earth and posterity—the heritage left to the generations who follow you.

Discover a new way of thinking about money and how to get a higher return on life itself—as you learn how to:

- Add posterity time to your busy schedule
- Best balance your career and family
- Invest in your children and grandchildren
- Include God in your financial planning
- Model a biblical attitude toward money for your children

You can make an eternal impact today when you learn to manage your money—and your life—well.

Russ Crosson, chief mission officer of Blue Trust, serves as chief advocate for the heart and soul of the organization and works to ensure the mission of the company is carried out with integrity in every area of the organization with a focus on making sure the company's mission is passed down and inculcated into future generations. With a background as president and CEO of Ronald Blue & Co. and executive director of the National Christian Foundation, Russ is dedicated to demonstrating how financial decisions can shape not just our current lives but our eternal futures.

For more information: bluetrust.com/books

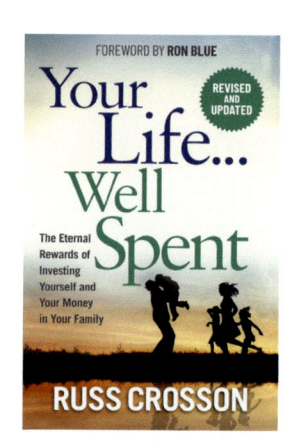

Email leverage@bluetrust.com to receive a complimentary copy of *Your Life...Well Spent*.

MORE BY KEN BOA

Recalibrate

NAVIGATING TRANSITIONS WITH PURPOSE AND HOPE

Living well doesn't happen automatically for followers of Christ—it happens when we have planned ahead by reviewing and recalibrating our lives on a regular basis, and when we transition from one stage of life to the next. Times of transition, especially in midlife or later life, are ideal moments for recalibrating our priorities and habits.

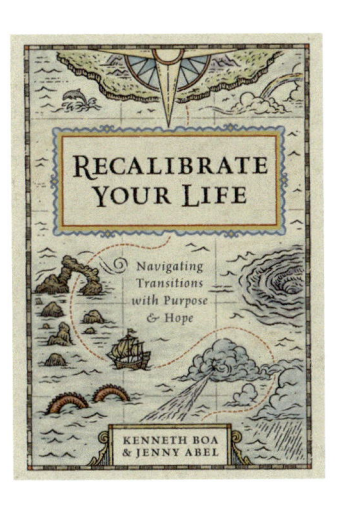

Ken Boa and Jenny Abel give us the perspective and practical tools needed to evaluate our God-given gifts, talents, skills, wisdom, knowledge, resources, and opportunities so we can use them to the full extent God desires. It involves an intentional recalibration and envisioning of one's life based on God's universal and unique purposes for each person as we move from the demands of our careers into a deeper sense of calling. This eternal perspective allows us to live meaningfully now and into the future so that the best is yet to come.

For more information: kenboa.org/recalibrate